# ALL THOSE MOMENTS

# ALL THOSE MOMENTS

## STORIES OF HEROES, VILLAINS, REPLICANTS, AND BLADE RUNNERS

# RUTGER HAUER
## WITH PATRICK QUINLAN

 HarperEntertainment

*An Imprint of HarperCollinsPublishers*

HarperCollins books may be purchased for educational, business, or sales promotional use. For information please write: Special Markets Department, HarperCollins Publishers, 10 East 53rd Street, New York, NY 10022.

FIRST EDITION

Title page photograph © 1982 Warner Brothers and the Blade Runner Partnership, courtesy of the Paul M. Sammon Collection.

*Designed by Mary Austin Speaker*

Library of Congress Cataloging-in-Publication Data has been applied for.

ISBN: 978–0–06–113389–3
ISBN–10: 0–06–113389-2

07 08 09 10 11 ID/RRD 10 9 8 7 6 5 4 3 2 1

*I've seen things you people wouldn't believe. Attack ships on fire off the shoulder of Orion. I watched C-beams glitter in the dark near the Tannhäuser Gate. All those moments will be lost in time, like tears in rain.*

# CONTENTS

*Rutger Hauer is contributing all of the money he earns from this book to the Starfish Association, an organization dedicated to helping people who live with AIDS and HIV.*

# ALL
# THOSE
# MOMENTS

# CHAPTER 1

## THE DAY MY WHOLE LIFE CHANGED

Which comes first, the belief or the success? I don't know. But you have to believe it's all going to work out. It's weird to say, but I've hardly ever been confident, and at the same time I've never really had a hard time making decisions. So somehow I must have felt confident enough.

*—RUTGER*

In early 2004, I had a problem.

I was in Los Angeles, and I had a job lined up that was keeping me in town—a small-budget movie that I thought was kind of interesting. It had something to do with a virus and the Internet and the fate of mankind. It seemed like it was all set, but then one of the financial backers suddenly disappeared. The producers called my agent, saying, "Well, we're not going to do the movie." This happened on a Thursday.

Now, disappointment is a way of life when you're in the movies. Sometimes you don't get the part you want, and sometimes a film you're in just dies. I've been in situations where I'm talking to my manager or agent, and I'll say, "What about that film we worked so hard on two years ago? When are we going to see that?" And it turns out the film died on the vine.

A backer pulled out and the film is not going to be released. The film is made, it's sitting on a shelf somewhere, and that's where it will continue to sit until the end of time. You have to be somewhat stoic about these things if you want to keep your sanity.

All the same, the early death of the virus movie came as a blow—I had been counting on it. The lease on my house in Santa Monica was up, and I had to decide if I was going to rent a house for another year. On the one hand, I couldn't be sure I'd get enough work during the year to justify it. On the other hand, although my primary home is in Holland, I need to have a base in the United States because I have a green card that I don't really feel like giving up.

"Oh, jeez," I said to myself. "What am I gonna do now?" It was a conundrum that could keep Einstein awake in his bed at night.

On Friday morning, I got another call from my agent.

"We have something really interesting."

"Let me guess," I said. "They're going to do this virus thing after all?"

"No. That would be good, but no. I think it's even better than that."

"Okay. I'm all ears."

"A young English director named Christopher Nolan is making a *Batman* movie in London. It's going to be sort of a more British version than the earlier ones, and he's interested in you for a part. Are you willing to travel, and if you are, will you travel quickly?"

"Let me read the script and I'll let you know."

My agent hesitated. "Okay, but you have to let me know by tonight."

"Tonight?"

"Tonight."

They sent a courier over with the script for *Batman Begins* early that afternoon. It was a totally different *Batman*, and had nothing to do with the earlier movies. In fact, it was a new beginning to the story. The character they were considering me for was Richard Earle, the CEO of Wayne Industries, who has made the company profitable by investing in arms deals and other sinister, under-the-table activities. It was a minor role, but I could see where I might have fun with it. In the story, he's the big boss, and the people who work for him snake around because they're a little afraid of him. He has that authority thing going on, and people want to get him, but they don't want to confront him directly. I thought the script, and the character, were really good.

The sun was just setting—the last light going out of the sky—as I called my agent back that evening.

"I like the script. So what's the deal?"

"Well," he said, "the deal is that they fly you to London very soon. And if they like you, you're working very soon. If they don't like you, you pay to fly yourself back to L.A., or to Amsterdam, or wherever you like, and you're not working."

Los Angeles to London is ten or eleven hours in the air. At least two and a half hours in the airport waiting to leave. Probably another two hours for a layover somewhere. Eight or nine hours lost to time-zone changes. A long journey by anyone's estimate—I could use a few days to prepare.

"When do they want me to fly?" I said.

"Tomorrow morning."

There was a pause on the line as I digested this latest information.

"Rutger?"

"Yes, yes. Fine. Tomorrow is fine."

I packed my bags in about twelve minutes—when you travel as much as I do, a lot of this stuff is just waiting to go, and the two bags I tend to travel with are solid and loyal companions. One is a Japanese designer's concoction, which is tougher than it looks and has already weathered the storms of several years. Nothing too fancy there—it holds clothes.

The other "bag" is a German trunk made out of aluminum. It is sooo strong. Not that it would do me much good, but it could survive anything—a plane crash, a nuclear war, you name it. It holds vitamins, a small weight for a specific exercise I need to do with one leg, and an ice-pack thing I need to use on the other leg when it has a busy day—the legacy of countless stumbles and falls during a career in action movies.

Scripts I should have read already are also in the trunk, along with cameras of various kinds. The DVD with a short film on it called *The Room* that I codirected, and which I enjoy showing people. It's in there. It also holds some books, some sweats, and some coins from the countries I visited last year rattling around at the bottom. Finally, there is the sophisticated Boy Scout knife for grown men—you'd be surprised at some of what I've been able to accomplish with that thing.

There was a time—before e-mail—when the trunk carried a small fax machine, just to be able to connect me home to my wife. Hard to believe, but it was only a few years ago when all of that connecting still needed to be organized by hand—in many a strange and exotic place, I used to tear my hotel room apart rewiring the phone hookup.

After packing up my stuff, I went right to bed, got up in the wee hours of Saturday morning, and flew to London. I felt pretty bleak—it was a long way to go if this director's "interest" turned out to be nothing.

Okay, I'm a doubter. Sometimes I hit a note, and the note is not doubtful. But so often we pretend to be gods in Gucci clothes, and it's nonsense. It's just to reassure ourselves and live in this illusion that we are solid as hell and we're not water, and we know what we're doing. We don't, and that's okay. If you know everything, then you're probably not open to new discoveries. What was the line from one of those Guinness commercials I did? "If you keep an open mind, you'll discover dark secrets."

I got to London very late Saturday night. By then, I barely remembered who I was or what I was doing there. People smiled at me in the airport—I smiled back. "Yes, hi. Hello." There was sparse traffic on the roads, so the car zipped to the hotel—a very nice place, classy furnishings, and a street-level suite. I hit the pillow and was gone in three minutes.

I woke up a few hours later in the grim light of an English dawn. It was Sunday morning, I had bloodshot eyes and enormous jet lag, and I got ready to see the director. As I stepped into the hallway of the hotel, I noticed Liam Neeson, the great actor from *Michael Collins* and many other films, standing there, several doors down. He was letting himself into his room. I knew he had a role in the movie. I had never met him, and if I got the part I wouldn't have any scenes with him, but

I had done a movie called *Past Midnight* with his wife, Natasha Richardson. That seemed like a good enough reason to intrude on his morning.

"Hey," I said. "Wait a minute, pal. Just let me say hi."

I came down there and we had a little chat. He had just come back from Iceland where he had shot most of his stuff. I said, "How is it going?" And he said, "Oh, you'll love it. It's really nice. The director is one of the best. But I'm so tired. I have to sleep." He said he had shot a fight scene on the ice that had taken the vinegar out of him. "Good for you," I said. I sent his wife my warm wishes, let him get to bed, and that was the end of that. Not even thirty-six hours had passed since I first read the script.

I met Christopher Nolan at a rented house outside London. He was there with his wife, two or three babies, and cardboard boxes piled everywhere. They were moving their stuff in. The shooting schedule had them traveling a lot, and they had only just flown in from Iceland themselves. We had a nice friendly breakfast together, and it turned out later that he was a big fan of Ridley Scott and *Blade Runner*—a director and a movie that are both close to my heart. Chris was twelve years old when *Blade Runner* first came out.

Chris and I talked for an hour and a half about the *Batman* movie, what he was trying to do with it, and my interpretation of the character. He said, "I want more character in this movie. I want more realism, instead of the usual high-tech fancy stuff." Of course, there would be plenty of high-tech stuff in the film—such as the Tumbler, the new version of the Batmobile, which was good fun and I think at least partially his own design—but I got his point. He wanted a movie that had less of a cartoon quality than the earlier ones.

As we finished up breakfast, I said, "Well, I really enjoyed our chat." I figured he'd talk to whoever else he had in mind for the part, check it all out with the producers, and then we'd see. I figured I'd head back to the hotel, get some more sleep, then spend the next day touring around London and waiting for an answer.

"I enjoyed it, too," he said. "What's tomorrow—Monday? You can start makeup and wardrobe tomorrow. Will that work for you?"

Just like that, I was on board *Batman Begins*, which would become one of the biggest movies of 2005. Chris had thrown me a long rope and said, "Okay, gamble with me." I took the gamble, and it paid off. Thirty-five years in a young, young industry, and I was still in business.

\* \* \*

My whole life changed the day I met Gerard Soeteman.

The year was 1968. Chris Nolan wouldn't be born for another two years. I was already a young man—twenty-four— and living in my native country, the Netherlands. I worked as a stage actor, my first job as a professional, and I was struggling just to make ends meet.

The province where I lived was rural north Holland. Wide-open blue sky, flat, sometimes gently rolling green farmland, windmills dotting the horizon, and empty roads disappearing into the distance. In the late 1960s, country living in the Netherlands meant isolation. Almost nobody had a telephone—if you wanted to talk to someone, you jumped on your bicycle and went to see them. A couple of buses passed each day. We were a three-hour drive from Amsterdam, but we were also worlds away.

The woman who would become my wife—Ineke—and I were just about broke. Each month, we made enough money to support ourselves for three weeks. The last week of the month was always tough. It was the basics we worried about. Did we have enough coffee and sugar? Who could we visit for a free dinner? Would the local cafeteria extend us some credit until the following week?

We lived in a tiny rented farmhouse along a dirt road, and we drew our water from the well with a hand pump—my morning shower was a bucket of cold well water. Our rent was low, and part of the deal was that I kept an eye on twenty or so noisy and coughing cows that were penned up on the property at night. The shit house was through the barn, out back—a little shack above steaming cow manure. We tended a small garden that would sometimes feed us for weeks at a time. Our living room had two beds built in the wall, which is how farm families once slept. In those early days, the workers would sleep in the kitchen, which was only separated by a wall from the cows—the body heat from the cows was a heating source. Each morning, I'd jump out of bed, race across the room, and jump even faster into my pants. Then I'd get three sweaters on and go make the coffee.

I was acting on the stage with the Noorder Compagnie, a tiny theater company bringing live performances to people in the towns and villages of Holland. We did the classics, like Shakespeare and Molière, and we also did more modern, groundbreaking plays, like *The Bald Soprano* by Eugène Ionesco. There were six of us in the cast, and we each did everything—set design and construction, costume design, makeup.

Our audiences adored us. They were country people and

to go to a show—even a show as small as ours—was their big night out. We were bringing live theater right to them, right to the rural countryside. And I mean rural—the rustic venues we played often smelled of cow shit. To get our government funding, we had to perform at least fifty times a year, but we would do a hundred or more shows because we were in such demand, making around 600 Guilders (or $300) a month. Multiply that by twelve and you have our yearly salary. Not much, but we were happy and poor.

We opened each play at the theater in our small town. It was a good, professional setting, and five hundred people would pour in to see our show. Then we would travel from town to town, performing in schools, in cafeterias, in town halls, even in parking lots. We would have a small caravan of two or three worn-out cars, each one packed with actors and equipment. In those days, I constantly changed cars, and so did my colleagues. The cars we had would break down all the time—the bodies would fall apart, the steering would go, there was always something wrong. I was a regular at the junkyard, looking for whatever I could afford that would run.

We soldiered on, bad cars and all, through snow and fog and rain and rutted, pitted country roads. We couldn't always find the venue right away, and sometimes we couldn't even find the town. To me, none of this was surprising, or even necessarily a hardship. Throughout history, actors have often been travelers and vagabonds. This was part of the heritage, a throwback to medieval days, when actors would travel from village to village on the backs of donkeys.

Culturally, not much had changed since those days, either. In Holland, acting was still frowned upon in many circles. The

Dutch value personal modesty—even today this is true. At that time, the entire profession of acting was looked upon as being a little bit strange, and probably unhealthy. How vain could you be to get up onstage and make a fool of yourself?

I won't say that acting was a dead end, but the best you could hope for was a steady paycheck, enthusiasm from the audience, and maybe a few positive lines from a writer in the local newspaper. Wealth and fame—these weren't even considerations. This was especially so for me because I was not a very good stage actor. I am a little shy—always have been—and I was not comfortable on the stage. Onstage, you have to make everything huge—grand, sweeping gestures, exaggerated facial expressions, vocalizations booming like cannon fire. You have to hurl your performance to the back of the theater, and I don't like to project myself that much.

On film, you make things smaller, more intimate. The distance you project is only the distance to the camera. That is your measuring tape. Film is a medium that likes to know less—it likes secrecy, and the smallest gesture can be significant. But I had no experience with film, and I didn't know what the problem was. I just had this vague notion—nothing I could put my finger on—that I was in trouble on the stage. I was giving my life to this effort, and I wasn't sure I could see much of a future in it. I was beginning to think I was in the wrong place, and that I was doing the wrong thing.

That's when Gerard Soeteman appeared.

He was a young television writer and producer, roving the countryside, making a series of short documentaries about arts in the provinces. He filmed us one day while we performed for children at a school. We were doing segments from three of

Shakespeare's plays—*As You Like It, The Taming of the Shrew,* and *Richard III.* The sword fighting grabbed his attention.

In Shakespeare's day, sword fighting—especially dueling to settle a grudge—was still in vogue. The actors had to know how to fence—otherwise the Globe Theatre groundlings would laugh them off the stage. But times have changed. In general, modern stage actors know little about swordplay. That's too bad, because even today, a good sword-fight scene can still make all the difference.

As luck would have it, I was good with a sword. At the age of thirteen, I had seen the great French actor Gérard Philipe play a swashbuckling sword fighter in the film *Fanfan la Tulipe,* and it inspired me to take up fencing. The sport became a passion of mine, and over the years I honed my skill. By my early twenties, I was far more confident about my ability with a rapier than I was about my acting.

After the performance, as the schoolchildren filed out of the small auditorium, Soeteman was waiting to speak with me.

"You did quite a job," he said. He seemed a serious man, already balding, in his late twenties or early thirties. He looked at me intently, studying me, as if measuring my size. "Tell me, can you also ride a horse?"

I shrugged. "Sure. I've been riding horses for years."

"Well, that's a happy coincidence. I'm writing a series for television. It's an adventure about a knight, kind of like Robin Hood, with a lot of horseback riding and sword fighting in the story. I think you might be a good fit for the lead. How would you feel about doing that sort of character?"

I shrugged. "Fine," I said, playing the game with him. "Let's do it." I didn't know what he was talking about. Television?

Dutch television was a fledgling industry—it hardly existed at all. There were about three TV stations in the whole country, and they would air three shows a night. During the day there was nothing on at all. You'd turn your TV set on and the screen was blank. We didn't even have a television at the farm—something like one out of every ten homes in the countryside had one.

TV was black-and-white, it wasn't the hottest item in town, and it was certainly not the window to the world. It was a toy in the corner of the room, something to watch on odd nights. What would entice anyone to watch it? There were only a handful of Dutch-made television shows, and the ones they did make were not terribly interesting to look at. Usually, they just pointed the camera at something and left it there.

"Okay," Soeteman said. "I'll talk to the director and see what he thinks. If he thinks it's a good idea, we'll contact you through the theater. You can come to Amsterdam and read for the part. Does that sound all right?"

"Sure. Good. I'll look forward to it."

By the next day, I had put the entire encounter out of my mind. The opportunity he described was too far outside my experience. He might actually be pulling together a TV show, but I doubted it would be any good, and I doubted very much that it would include me.

\*       \*       \*

Soeteman contacted me a month later. He sent me part of a script, and I thought what I read was fantastic. As I drove into Amsterdam for the audition, the ancient buildings, bridges, and canals of my home city all seemed like new to me. My wires were buzzing and humming with excitement, even confidence.

The story was called *Floris,* and was loosely based on the life of Count Floris V, a figure from Dutch medieval history. His ancestral land was stolen from him when he was very young, and he had returned to claim it. This was a role that seemed written with me in mind. I'd be able to use my fencing and my horse-riding abilities—it smelled like a great way to be an actor. I knew I could fence. I knew I could ride a horse. How difficult could it be?

That morning, I met the director for the first time. He was Paul Verhoeven, wild-eyed, crazy with energy, barely older than myself. This was the man who would one day go on to direct *Robocop, Total Recall, Basic Instinct,* and a host of other great American action films. He was fresh from the Dutch army, where he had been making training films and documentaries—*The B Company Finds a Problem in the South,* and that sort of thing. He had stood out because at the time, whatever they did in the army was usually kind of sluggish and stupid, but everything he did, he did it with tremendous, almost frantic vigor.

"With this show," he told me, "we are either going to succeed or we are going to fail. But whatever we do, we're going to do it on a grand scale."

We got together at the headquarters of the film company. Even this was a step beyond anything I had seen before—they had an office with a desk, a phone, and a filing cabinet, and some studio space in back. They had some camera equipment and makeshift wooden scenery that gave you the sense of being out in the countryside somewhere in medieval times.

They had a boom man, a microphone guy, and some lights. They even had business cards.

It was a professional setup, and I came away from the experience feeling powerfully optimistic. Verhoeven and I clicked from the beginning. I felt I knew what he wanted and could deliver it almost before he asked for it. On the drive back to the north of the country, I had no doubt that I was the man for the part.

The man they picked was named Carol van Herwignen. I probably would have been upset to hear about this, but I never did—not until a long time later. Van Herwignen—who to this day is still a working actor in Holland—turned down the role. He was under some time constraints, and on the off chance that shooting ran over schedule—two months was the plan— he would have to leave the show for another commitment.

I was the also-ran, the second best, but I didn't know it. My ignorance was a blessing because it made me confident—I felt that no matter what happened, I would be the best on a horse and the best with a sword.

We did the show with the lightest touch. Jos Bergman played my sidekick, a wizard from India named Sindala. My character was straitlaced, almost comically so, and his character would do tricks and gaze into the future. We shot entirely on location in the Dutch and Belgian countryside, at places like the ancient and brooding Castle Doornenburg. We worked outside, on horseback, in full medieval costume, with a director who was full of energy and excitement.

I did many of my own stunts, and sometimes I would surprise them—give them a little scare. One time, the stunt was that I was supposed to run along the top of the castle, find a gap in the wall, and leap three stories into the moat. When the time came, I dove instead—into only eight feet of water.

Verhoeven applauded. "That's good, Rutger," he said. "Break your neck. It'll make for better footage."

If acting in films was going to be a new life for me, there was no better way to start. The opening day of shooting was like a celebration, a rejoicing. From the moment I stepped in front of the camera, I fell in love. I felt that film was my medium and that I was finally in the right place. As the shooting progressed, I resolved that I was going to try very hard to make this, rather than stage acting, my profession. I was like a child—we all were. We were all doing it for the first time. Everybody was learning, everybody was on their toes, going, "This is bigger than we thought. Wow, can we handle it?"

Of course, the filming went slower than planned—much slower. The project was hugely ambitious in a country where this sort of thing just wasn't done, and the two months scheduled for filming became four months, then dragged on to six months. Simple problems would screw up the shoot. Equipment broke and pieces of it flew through the air. Costumes fell apart. The horses would go left when they were supposed to go right, and it would take half a day to discover what had distracted them. Was it the lights? Was it the microphone? In every sword fight, somebody would forget the choreography, and the director would be there, screaming, "Keep going! Keep going!" When shooting was finally finished, we had spent 300 percent of our original budget.

After the shoot, I returned to my normal life on the stage. Indeed, I had never left. Throughout most of the filming, I raced back and forth across the country, shooting *Floris* in the daytime and appearing in plays at night. The film company had hired a car to drive me, and I did much of my sleeping in the backseat as we rolled along the highways. But with *Floris* done, I embarked on a quiet time, sort of a period of withdrawal. It was like, you've flown so high, and now you go back to the life you really live. Several months passed, maybe even a year, before the show was ever aired.

I remember how Ineke and I went to her parents' house to catch that first episode. We settled on the carpet around the TV, and we waited. I felt a nervous anticipation, a sinking feeling in my stomach. I suspected that we had done a good job, but I had never seen the finished product.

I was not prepared for what I saw when the show came on—or for the reaction to it from the public. In the weeks ahead, word of the program would spread, and the highways would be empty on Sunday evenings as the entire country gathered to watch the first smash-hit TV show in Dutch history.

# CHAPTER 2

## "LONG LIVE WINSTON CHURCHILL!"

You might say I was born into acting. You might say that, but for a long time it didn't seem to be the case.

I came into this world on January 23, 1944, near Amsterdam. It was the tail end of World War II and the Nazi occupation of the Netherlands. On May 10, 1940, Nazi Germany had attacked my native country without warning. Despite heroic efforts from the Dutch military, the Germans won the fight in just five days. The German air force, the dreaded Luftwaffe, bombed Rotterdam, our second largest city, to rubble. No one knows for sure how many people died in that attack, but it is thought to be in the thousands. The Luftwaffe specialized in the Shock and Awe of its time, and it worked. The Dutch government surrendered to spare the country the horror of another Rotterdam.

Queen Juliana and the royal family of Holland—the House
of Orange—escaped to exile in England. During the five years
of occupation, the Germans shipped more than a hundred
thousand Jews living in the Netherlands to death camps in
Germany, Poland, and other parts of Europe. The most famous
of these was a girl named Anne Frank.

If you've ever seen a film I did for American TV called
*Escape from Sobibor,* you may remember a scene in which a passenger train loaded with well-dressed Dutch Jews—back then
people dressed their best when they traveled, and in the film
these travelers seem unaware of their fate—pulls up to the
Sobibor death camp. More than thirty-four thousand Dutch
Jews were deported to Sobibor alone. Of these, only two indi-
viduals are thought to have survived.

Near the end of the war, conditions in Holland got very
bad. The Nazis confiscated Dutch food and fuel to use in their
failing war effort, and food supplies in Dutch cities soon ran
out. The winter of 1944–1945, when I was one year old, is
known as "the Hunger Winter." More than thirty thousand
Dutch starved or froze to death by the time of the liberation
in May 1945.

I was too small to remember any of this. My first recollec-
tions come at four or five, after the war was over. However, the
devastating memories of the war were bright in the minds of
everyone around me. In my earliest days, we were poor and we
lived on a small farm outside of Amsterdam. I'm told we had a
goat and I was fed on fresh goat's milk for my first few years.
My parents, Arend and Teunke, were actors, but there was no
work for actors right after the war—nobody had the money to

pay for a theater show. Those years were hard on most families, and we were no exception.

After a short time, we moved to Breukelen, an industry town just south of Amsterdam. The borough of Brooklyn in New York City is named for Breukelen—New York City itself was once known as New Amsterdam, after the Dutch settled there in the 1600s. In Breukelen, the real memories of my childhood begin.

I remember it as a happy time. We were very poor, but it didn't bother me. Being poor didn't have any meaning back then. You didn't have to own certain clothes or a specific pair of shoes. There was food on the table, and we had some clothes, and we were fine. Everybody around us was in the same boat, so we didn't know we were missing anything.

Our home was an apartment on the fourth floor of a building above the Amstel Canal. There was a shipping business underneath where we lived. I mean this literally—we lived upstairs from a loading dock. On the floors below us were the freight offices, and below that was the dock. A little trolley rolled on train tracks across the yard, carrying the heavy cargo that would go out to the dock. The ships were smaller cargo vessels—eighty to a hundred feet long—but to my young eyes they were gigantic. The ships were built for domestic runs, sailing to ports in other parts of Holland. There was a constant hustle and bustle of men working and shouting, ships coming in, ships going out, whistles, bells, horns, always something going on, from early morning until night, and all of it just outside my window.

The activity fascinated me. The Dutch have always been

sailors, and the Amstel has long been their artery to the world. Like many of my countrymen before me, the sea called to me from my earliest childhood. I wanted to be out there, not just working on the docks, but sailing the seas. As I grew older, depending on who the skippers were, I was on the docks, helping the workmen with smaller loads, running errands, and just getting to know that world—the world of ships. I'm sure I was a pest, but I must have been a good pest, because nobody chased me off. In fact, at the age of ten I sailed on one of these cargo ships for the first time. The captain was leaving for a short trip, and I asked him if could go.

I can see him now, a big man, frowning, hesitating for a long moment.

There was no way he would let me go—how could he? He was busy. He had responsibilities. He didn't need some kid underfoot.

"Get on," he said, and my heart leaped.

I don't remember where we went, but it mustn't have been very far. We went by day and were back at home that same night.

When I wasn't prowling the docks, I was in the water. Swimming has always been one of my favorite activities. In Amsterdam, the other children and I would build rafts, float them out into the canals, and dive off of them. These were the days when raw sewage was released directly into the canals— before environmental protections for water.

We swam with the shit flushed from thousands of toilet bowls, and the gasoline and the oil skids trailing behind the big ships. To us, it was a joke. "Hi, how ya doing?" we'd say to the next batch of toxic sludge flowing by. It was probably unhealthy, and the thought of it might give modern parents nightmares, but it doesn't seem to have harmed me any. I'm still here, in any case.

While I was off sailing and swimming in polluted canals, my parents were away from home much of the time. A few years after the war ended, they started getting work as actors again, and that work took them to other parts of the country and even other parts of the world.

The first trip I remember them taking was a major one—they went to Indonesia, halfway around the globe, for about six months. They had to travel by boat and it took a long time. It was an artist exchange between the Netherlands and Indonesia, which in those days was still a Dutch colony.

There were three children in the family at that time—myself, my sister Karen, who was seven years older than me, and my sister Machteld, who was two years younger than me. My youngest sister, Brigitta, was not yet born. When our parents left for Indonesia I was not even speaking yet. When they came back, I gave them a hearty greeting—one of my very first sentences, and a passionate ode to the leader of England during the war:

"Long live Winston Churchill!"

The troubling thing here is that my parents left their children behind. I don't understand why they did that. I never talked to them about it later in life, or even felt bad about it. I just accepted it—it was how things were. But if I look at it now, I sometimes think, "Who would do that kind of thing?" They left us behind until I was probably about three years old. Machteld was still a baby.

After the trip to Indonesia, my parents were often on the

road. Once they started working, and had steady work, they were off somewhere most of the time, and a young woman, our nanny, would take care of us while Karen was less a sister than her assistant. She had a lot of responsibility at a tender age. She had to look after us no matter what happened, and frankly, Machteld and I were not easy to handle. We were partners in crime. Who could control us? We were like a swarm of stinging gnats, a herd of raging buffalo. It's sad. I think Karen was shaped by that experience for the rest of her life.

The nanny was a dancer, as was the seventeen-year-old girl who would also fill in for her sometimes. I grew up with a lot of dancing girls around. Karen was another one of them. The three of them—the nanny, the teenage girl, and Karen—all wanted to become professional dancers, practicing so hard and for so long that their toes would bleed.

It was serious classical ballet. "Girls' stuff" is how I thought of it. They had to train for hours every day, and watching them, I learned that dancers must be addicted to pain. If they don't feel pain, they think there's something wrong. And in the end, Karen never quite made it in the ballet. She was not built right—she was too short and too wide. Her body was too strong, and her bones were too thick. In classical ballet, that doesn't quite work. She wasn't a tiny flower that the male dancers could throw around. She was motivated, and very willing to endure the pain, but in the long run, that wasn't enough.

Meanwhile, I came to know my often-absent parents in bits and pieces. My mother was a volcano. She was a beautiful woman with American Indian features and sharp eyes and incredible energy—she couldn't stay still. She would ride a moped with our pet dachshund in the side of her bag, its snout sticking out as it watched the scenery go by. She would go to the market that way, shopping for food, all at the last minute before dinner. She moved like there was music playing some-where that only she could hear. She would sing in the kitchen. Both she and my father were well educated and artsy, intellec-tuals who read an enormous amount and swayed to the music at all hours of the night.

My father was a handsome man, tall and athletic with amazing blue eyes that made women go crazy, but life with him was hard. We couldn't seem to reach each other. He used to hide in his head, which is a great trick. If you didn't understand him, you might think, "What's wrong with this guy?" You'd be doing something, or saying something, and there would be no response coming from him. Physically he was there, but mentally he was out to lunch. Then one day he would be back again and he would try to make it up. He did some good things during these makeup times. Once, we built a canoe together, or that's how he would describe it: "We built a canoe together." But even that meant he built a canoe and I got to play with it when it was ready.

Of course, with no parents around most of the time, it was up to me how often I went to school. I played hooky a lot. I felt that life was so interesting and intense, and school was bor-ing, so why go? My only urge at the time was "If I'm outside, I'm good." And it wasn't because the school itself was bad, or I was bad. It was just that I loved it outside. That's where the magic was. I have always been a sensualist, feeling everything, absorbing everything. I loved the city, with its bridges, its tree-lined thoroughfares, and its antique architecture. I loved the ships. I loved the canals, even in winter when they were frozen over. I loved the small lakes around the city.

School simply couldn't compare. Whenever I was in school, I longed to be outside. The same scenario would play itself out, over and over. We would be in class, and the teacher would be in the front, droning on about something or another. And my mind would drift. Soon the lesson, the teacher, the other children, the classroom itself would be gone. And a bird might fly outside the window, sailing against a pale blue sky.

"Rutger?" a stern voice would say.

The bird would float there on the wind. Beautiful. Impossible.

"Rutger!" The stern voice, raised now, would rip me back to reality.

"Yes?"

"The answer, please."

As always, hesitant, embarrassed giggles came from the other children. "What was the question again?" I'd say, my face turning red.

I did have one great teacher who showed me a lot of patience and generosity. We called him Master Dekema. He was tall and thin and severe, almost in the manner of Ichabod Crane. He could have killed me a hundred times over. He could have thrown me out of the school. Instead, he took me under his wing. Master Dekema would punish me in front of the class often enough—because I didn't do my homework, or because I acted up in some way. He would say, "You have to stay after school and write a hundred lines on the blackboard." After school, in the quiet classroom, I would begin to write the lines. Ten minutes later, when everybody was gone, he would look up from his desk.

"Well, shall we go?"

Then he would put me on his bicycle and drop me off at home. He knew there were often no parents at our home, so he took Machteld and me on skating trips from time to time. He was like a mentor to me. I knew him until I was twelve or so, the whole six years I was in that school. After that, when I was a man, I hoped I would run into him again somewhere, and let him know how much I appreciated the way he had treated me back in school.

Thankfully, the school year didn't last forever. Once a year, during summer holidays, the whole family would travel to the island of Schiermonnikoog in the northeast of the country. It is the smallest of the five Dutch Wadden Islands, the last piece of land between Holland and Norway on Holland's north coast.

The island has national-park status now, and three hundred thousand guests visit each year. During my childhood, it was decidedly less crowded, and our trips there fed my thirst for adventure. The farther you wandered from the ferry landing, the more you became part of an unspoiled paradise. Seals would loll on the rocks and frolic in the water. Sand dunes looked over some of the widest beaches in Europe—at low tide it could take forever to cross the vast sands. The winds forever blew. Seagulls flew and called overhead.

For me, this was, and remains, an innocent, ideal place. We stayed in an old whaler's house, which had been built two centuries before and looked out to sea. From morning to night, I just roamed and enjoyed myself. In the morning, before first light, I would get up and accompany the milkman on his rounds. I would handle and ride the horse that was there. I would swim in the ocean every day. The only sad part about being there was leaving when the holiday ended.

I had an uncle who would drive us up to the ferry terminal on the mainland. He used to let me drive the car, starting when I was ten or twelve years old. There were not many cars in Holland in those days, so there was very little traffic. The whole family would be in the car, and he would sit me up in his lap and let me steer along a lovely stretch of road that had many curves. I'd be yelling "Faster! Faster!" It gave both my parents heart attacks every time.

As time passed while in school, we saw a few movies every week. I was crazy for westerns. They were about tough guys, and I've never been a tough guy in real life. I was not a tough kid—I didn't have to be. I grew early and was much bigger than all the other kids, so I didn't ever have to fight. I was just this huge, good-natured, gentle giant. I was so big and square-bodied that when the other kids would have an argument, they'd just go, "Rutger!" Then I would just go where the action was, give them all a smile, and that would be the end of it. In real life, there was no sense in actually fighting about anything, but in my imagination, when watching a western, tough looked pretty cool.

When I was thirteen, I saw a movie that changed how I spent my time. This was *Fanfan la Tulipe,* a French film starring the great actor Gérard Philipe. It came out in 1952, but I didn't see it until several years later. Philipe played a musketeer, a dashing hero who gets conscripted into the French army. It was lightweight fun, and I decided I wanted to be like the man I saw in this movie, riding horses and fencing like a maniac. Philipe was the European James Dean—he was handsome and he died much too young. I took up horseback riding and fencing at age thirteen.

Before long, my childhood came to an end. Sometime after my fifteenth birthday I decided I was done with home and done with school. I had been held back in school so I felt like a grown man, sitting in a classroom with children. In fact, I was bigger physically than the teachers.

I wasn't acting up, and I would do a bit of homework, but I thought it was boring and knew I would have to work really hard to finish high school. I would rather be in the streets, ogling the pretty girls. I didn't know what I was doing in school, in Amsterdam, even in the Netherlands. The world was a big place, and I felt trapped. My parents—who by then were acting teachers in Amsterdam, and were home much more often—were reaching a point of despair with me.

My mother's family knew somebody in the shipping industry, and since my earliest days, I had always loved the sea. Deep down inside, I knew the way out.

One day I said to my mother, "Can I not go sail?"

# CHAPTER 3

## LIFE AT SEA

"Hauer! Mop those decks! Get moving!"

At the age of fifteen, I signed on to work as a mate on the freighter *Fabian* in the Dutch Merchant Navy—a twelve-thousand-ton container ship that was scheduled to travel the world. I would be the youngest man on ship, and lowest man on the totem pole—carrying out the most menial service tasks. The only way I would ever command that ship was if everybody else died. In the days before I left, I had no second thoughts. Instead, I felt a tremendous sense of "This is it. This is what I've been waiting for. I am finally starting out as a man." There were no tearful farewells. I boarded that ship with my eyes on the future, and no looking back.

I spent my first week at sea throwing up.

The morning we left Amsterdam, it was a nice day, sunny,

with very little wind and hardly a cloud in the sky. Within an hour, my face was green, and I was leaning over the rail, painting the side of the ship with my insides. I was like that for a week, and it was just beautiful weather. The motion itself was enough to make me sick—just the sea going gently up and down. After I got used to it, things were a little better. But every time we hit a storm, every time we hit water, or weather, that was stronger than I'd known so far, I would be sick again.

There were about fifty men on the *Fabian,* and the ship itself was about a hundred and fifty yards long. Out in the vastness of the ocean, the ship was its own little world. And it was further divided into three more little worlds. The sailors were Dutch. The laundrymen were Chinese—it was a custom that the Chinese did laundry on these ships. And finally, the cook and his few kitchen staff were Indonesian.

There wasn't much interaction between the Dutch guys on the ship and the Chinese guys. To some extent, this was because of the language barrier. They spoke Chinese and we didn't. We spoke Dutch and they didn't. It's amazing that it worked out at all, but it did. We'd speak a little English, and they would have about three words of English, and that was about as much as we connected. We would hardly ever see them, except when they picked up the laundry, which happened once a week.

At the back of the boat was where the sailors lived. Most of the tiny cabins slept two men each, and then there was a mess room that held twenty for breakfast. There were only three teenagers on the boat, and the three of us all slept in one cabin. I was fifteen, the next oldest was sixteen, and then there was one eighteen-year-old guy. He was a big guy—huge—and he seemed so much older than we were. Even more, he was always dirty and he had weird hours because he worked in the engine room. He would have to work through the night and then he would come back to the room totally filthy, smelling of oil and sweat and grime. It was all very romantic.

The food was terrible. Almost everything came from a can. When we pulled into port, things would look up a little bit. The ship would buy fresh eggs, fruits and vegetables, and chicken or other meat—whatever was available. The fresh food would come aboard, we would stow it, and when we were at sea, in a short while it would be gone again. Then it was back to the canned stuff.

My tasks were grunt work—mopping floors, cleaning, painting, doing a little bit of the night watch, getting coffee ready, bringing the breakfast in the morning. It was glorified maid's work. And it never ended. There were always chores that needed to be done, and there was always someone on my case, ready to give me something more to do. Within a short time, I learned to appreciate the job of a housewife. Such an endless series of mindless, tedious work. When one job was done, another would begin. I worked hard, like nothing I had known before. I was tired most of the time, filled with a sense that I was far from home, and there was nobody to help me. I became committed to doing my job to the best of my ability. Once I could keep up the pace, then I could open my eyes to the vast world we were traveling through.

We went to America first. We sailed across the Atlantic

Ocean to the east coast of North America, then down the St. Lawrence River, through the Great Lakes, passing the cities of Quebec, Montreal, Milwaukee, Detroit, and Chicago. All these lakes, so big they seemed like oceans themselves.

I remember coming to Chicago and being blown away. The Big Shoulders—building upon building, stretching out away from the lake, towering concrete canyons. It was huge, frenzied, and fast-paced. I walked the streets, little more than a boy dressed as a sailor. At each streetlight, logjams of people would wait on the corners. There were signs everywhere, flashing messages. I rode the elevator to the observatory of one of the buildings, got way on top just to see what it was like. Far away, I could see great ships on the lake, traffic moving on the roadways, and below me, swarms of people scurrying like termites. This was as close to the sky as I had ever been. Forty stories, fifty stories, sixty stories. Each building was bigger than the one before.

Amsterdam was a quiet place in comparison. The Netherlands, at that time, didn't have any buildings bigger than maybe seven and a half stories. In Chicago it was all so *big*. America was rich. America was dynamic. America was the land of opportunity. While I felt I had known about America, I really hadn't. It is one thing to hear about something, or read about it, but it is something quite different to experience it. I got a flavor on my tongue that made me say to myself, "Wow. This is the place to be. Will I ever come back here?"

From Chicago, we sailed back the way we came, across the ocean to Gibraltar, Barcelona, Italy, down the Suez Canal to the Indian Ocean, to the Persian Gulf, then all the way to Ceylon—which is now known as Sri Lanka—and Pakistan.

Then we pressed on to Southeast Asia, as far as Saigon. It was marvelous. Everything was strange to me. My mates and I would walk the streets and alleys, people shouting and calling in languages I had never heard, cuts of meat hanging in the open air, and food cooking in stalls. I might buy a piece of food on the street, carrying out the transaction with hand gestures. "That. Yes, that. Two?" Two fingers in the air. "Yes, two of these coins for that piece of meat. That's what he means. Yes." And I would taste the food and say to my mate, "I have never tasted anything like this before . . . It's quite delicious. Maybe it's chicken."

We were always in the seedy parts of town. Imagine you're fifteen years old, you're with two mates little older than yourself, halfway around the world from where you started, surrounded by a culture starkly different from your own, and transacting in a language you neither speak nor understand. You could be from another planet, another world. Soon enough, you discover that the rules are very different in each country, that you don't know the rules, and you're never in any one place long enough to discover what they are. So you go to a seedy bar and you drink yourself stupid. Then it becomes a matter of stumbling back to the ship through warrens and alleyways that become more confusing with each step. Before the end of that trip, I had decided it was silly to go from harbor to harbor, spending time in bars. I wasn't the best drinker anyway.

What was most startling, and made the deepest impression on me, was the poverty. I saw all these different countries, and everywhere I went, I saw poverty that just didn't exist in Holland. There were people with no food. People living in tiny ramshackle homes, packed together, built from throwaway junk, and people with nowhere to live. Swarms of hungry children in ragged clothes, begging for a little spare change. Crippled people, people with serious illnesses, people with no hope in their eyes, begging for help and dragging themselves along. I would see all this with my own eyes, and then we would sail on to the next port.

When the ship was at sea, we sometimes encountered tremendous storms. I loved the heavy weather. One time, we were out at sea, and it was storming like something out of a nightmare. We were waiting for the waves to calm down enough so that we could safely enter this tight harbor. The waves were fifty to sixty feet high, and our ship was being thrown around. Its bow would dive into each wave, and the ship would ride and lift out of the wave, all the way until it was right at the top. Then it would come crashing down into the next. If you've seen *The Perfect Storm,* then you know what I'm talking about. That film does a good job of showing at least what this looks like.

One night, during such a storm I got an idea. I left our cabin and crawled across the front deck, holding on to safety lines, until I reached the front of the boat. Once there, I held myself to a railing, and rode these big waves. Sometimes the water broke over the bow on top of me. The force of the sea was unimaginable, and the engineering of that boat was just as incredible—that it could stay there in that rough sea and survive. The whole thing was amazing. This didn't last long because my superiors saw me out there and shouted through the speakers on deck, "What the fuck? Get your ass back here! Are you crazy?"

All my life, there's been something that pushes me to

the edge. There's an element of discovery to it. I'm a curious person. I always want to see what's over the next hill. I wanted to feel the power of that storm—as a result, I learned to respect it.

Life at sea was good—more than I even thought it was going to be. Before I left, I was hoping that if I liked it, I could find a way to do more work like this. But I'm color-blind. When you're a sailor, you can't be color-blind because you have to steer the boat a couple of hours a day and you have to be able to recognize the different colored lights on the buoys. You can't go up in rank if you can't do this. There are jobs you *can* do—you can go in the engine room, for instance. But in the engine room, when I've tried it—that's not half as exciting. You're covered with oil, and surrounded by noise. Anyway, I love standing on deck and watching the waves.

As it happens, my great-grandfather on my mother's side was the captain of a schooner, and he was also color-blind. A century and a half ago, the beacons at night were fires. But when the modern era came, they changed the fires into colored lights. The moment that happened, they took his ship away, because he couldn't see the difference. So I realized I couldn't be a commercial skipper. Even so, I had just had my sixteenth birthday, and had already seen more of the world than many people would see in their lifetimes.

The homecoming was a non-event. We had one really big storm and had to wait almost a day to enter the harbor. I came off the ship at about eleven o'clock in the morning and I just went home. There was no big dramatic meeting at the dock. As I walked along my street, the house seemed smaller than I had pictured it.

That, and when I walked inside, the place seemed so messy.

I thought, "Oh, look at this place. I'll help a little bit here." So I put down my bags and started cleaning the house. I had hardly ever picked up anything before I left.

My mother stood in the doorway, stunned, and smiling.

# CHAPTER 4

## RUDE AWAKENINGS

Back at home in Holland after nearly a year at sea, life was a series of rude awakenings.

It wasn't long before I was back into the daily grind. I had all sorts of jobs during the day to make some money. For a while, I worked in a factory that made lights for the theater. A friend of my father's owned the place, and they had a temporary vacancy. I learned how to weld there, and I learned how to work with steel. I liked it there a lot and was sad when that job ended—it was great to work with my hands. Later, I painted sets for the opera for three or fours months. Because I'm color-blind, they had to sort of go, "Okay, you take that can of paint and paint that wall, and take that can there and paint that . . ."

Three nights a week I went to school. The idea was for

me to finish high school—I had gone off to sea without ever graduating. I would go to school after a day of work, when I was already tired, and I would fall asleep in class. But I was committed to finishing, and I am glad I went. My time at sea had taught me the importance of speaking different languages, and in school I was able to take language classes. So I began to add languages to the Dutch, Frisian, and English I already had—I studied German, French, and Italian. I did that for two years and finally graduated high school.

It was during this time at home that I noticed my relationship with my parents had changed. When we kids were young they used to mock us a lot because what we were doing was pretty silly most of the time. *Mock* may be a strong word here—it usually took the form of a gentle teasing. But that's not always what you need from them. So I remember a day when I looked at my father—I didn't even say anything—I just looked at him and silently mocked him back. It was about some little thing that I don't even recall. I just remember how I looked at him, and how he looked at me.

I was seventeen, and I was suddenly a son who's going "What the fuck, man? Cut the crap. I know you've been doing it this way for fifty years, but you could change, you know. It's not that hard." It was totally nonverbal between my dad and me. He opened his eyes wide in surprise, as if he was seeing me for the first time. Then he stared at me and it was like he was thinking, "Uh-oh. Rutger's getting older."

But I think there was also love there, and understanding. My parents knew that as my schooling ended, I was struggling with what I would do next. They were actors, so they said,

"Why don't you try acting school? If you don't like it you can stop."

My parents were not well-known actors in terms of mainstream fame, but at that time, nobody in Holland really was. After the war ended, several more years passed before the theater really revived itself and there was a new future in acting. By then, my parents were in their forties. The problem was my father was the beautiful guy, the lover. And that kind of actor, the dashing, handsome devil—after thirty years old that starts to fade, and by forty, it doesn't really sit anymore. My mother had the same problem—if beauty can be considered a problem. The real problem was that the war had derailed the theater for nearly ten years, and my parents missed their peaks. My father did some character work, but then the theater company that he loved working for went under.

After that, my parents stopped working in the traditional way as actors and they decided to teach people how to act. They taught in the acting school in Amsterdam for about six years. As a teenager, I visited the school and watched them when they taught, and I even worked with them a few times. I don't think I understood what they were trying to teach me. You would pretend to be somebody else and then do all kinds of tricks, and it was kind of exciting.

So I agreed with them.

In the fall, I enrolled in theater school. I had high hopes, but from the very first, it didn't work out. I could never show up for school on time. Sometimes I didn't show up at all. At eight o'clock in the morning, I just couldn't make it. I had three clocks and I would sleep straight through the alarms. It wasn't that I was working at night and my busy schedule rendered me unable to wake up. I wasn't doing anything outside of school. I just wanted to sleep. Meanwhile, the school felt that acting was a craft demanding seriousness and hard work.

After three months, they threw me out.

At that time, in the early 1960s, service in the Dutch military was compulsory for all young men. I knew that at some point, I would have to go in for a year and a half. By then I was eighteen, old enough to join, and after crapping out of drama school, I figured now was a good time to get my patriotic duty out of the way. So I joined the army. And it was great fun—for a little while.

I was stationed at an army base a few hours outside Amsterdam. It was me and a lot of young raw recruits just like myself. Our first two months was a time when our overseers put us through our paces to see how fit we were and who could do what. It was all just a great big physical workout.

Every day, we had to run five miles before breakfast. After breakfast, we'd spend the day doing all kinds of exercises—obstacle courses, swinging on ropes, swimming, and whacking one another with big pugel sticks. And there were more specific trainings. This was the medical corps and I was training to become a medic, so they would have us carry out exercises designed to mimic that kind of work. The idea was we would run out in combat with stretchers. We had to crawl a hundred yards with a guy on our back. One of my comrades would drape himself over my back, and I would crawl along, low to the ground, dodging the imaginary bullets that were whistling overhead, with him on top of me. It was heavy, tiring, muscle-burning work.

Whatever we did, I always came in first, and I was having a lot of fun with it. I loved any physical activity they made us do—and what I loved most of all was the marching. They would put us all together and teach us how to march around on the parade ground. All of us, the whole battalion, all moving together. In a short time, we began to march with amazing harmony and prowess. It was almost like a dance, with its own sort of beauty.

But two months pass very quickly. And in the next two months, things started to change. The thing is, in the military, they train you to kill. That's what the exercise is all about. I was supposed to become a medic, but what I was training to do most of the time was to kill people. They had us shooting and doing the typical exercises—for example, charging with a bayonet and stabbing dummies. And I thought, "Well, in the movies that's fine, but in real life, that's not too good. Only a madman would want to do that."

Then they would show us movies of how tough it could get for us. They had all this footage that either they had staged, or someone had actually taken during battle. It was black-and-white footage. Funny, crazy, strange little movies. But not pleasant.

I started to realize that this wasn't all just having a great time and a physical workout. They really meant for us to kill somebody if and when they told us to. I didn't want to kill anyone, and certainly not on demand—simply because someone else told me to.

To make matters worse, during the next two months I was in training to become a sergeant. I was going to have a bunch of army groupies to do what I commanded and follow me. It just wasn't the right place for me. I thought, "Hey, a sane man cannot be here, and I think I'm sane, so I think I should try and get out."

So I had a nervous breakdown. Of sorts.

One fine day, I escaped. I climbed over the wall of the base and went to see a friend of the family—an older man who was a doctor and was also in the army. No doubt he was surprised when I appeared at his home. I asked him for some advice, and he said, "You gotta crawl right back in there. If you stay out more than twenty-four hours, they will put you in prison."

Prison didn't sound appealing, so I went back. When I arrived, I told my superiors that I was having problems. Big problems. I was depressed. I was hearing voices. Maybe I was seeing things—I didn't know. I was trying to convince them that I was mentally unfit for duty. It was a big job, that's for sure. Two months earlier, they had awarded me best soldier of the battalion in terms of fitness. Physically, I was the best of the bunch, so it was difficult for them to grasp this sudden onset of insanity.

When you were in the army, and you had gone insane, they would feed you into this bureaucratic system, which would swallow you and then pass you along like a morsel of food. First, you had to speak to a medical doctor. Then you had to speak to a psychiatrist, and then you had to speak to a board of psychiatrists, all sitting at a long table and staring at you. If all of that went one way, you would go back into the military. If it went another way, you would go . . . well, they had several methods to deal with that. The method that was the funniest was if they didn't know quite what to do with you, they would park you in a halfway-crazy house where everybody was just waiting. This was what happened to me.

They were trying to evaluate who was actually crazy and who could just be released back into society. It was like a parking lot for crack-up cases. Army accidents. The gay guys. The nutty guys. And the guys who really did have mental problems. They were there, too. I was there for two weeks. I was pretty much on my own, and I had a good time. I was isolated and alone on this big campus, but there was a library. So I would read beautiful Russian literature in the woods all day. In the morning, after breakfast, I would just go out to a spot in the woods, and take a few books, and come back at the end of the day.

The surroundings were lovely and the stories were wonderful, and I felt at ease. Now and then I'd have to have another talk with one of the psychiatrists. That happened each Monday and Wednesday. I would tell them that I was depressed and that I was lonely, that I had conflicting feelings about killing people and that I was scared. I told them that I had these terrible headaches. The only problem was I had never had headaches before, so I had to figure out a way to get in character. I slammed my head into a tree a few times to feel what a headache was like. That was the first moment that I went, "Oh, this must be Method acting."

After all of that reading and acting, each Friday they decided who had to stay and who could leave. The weekends were the worst part because absolutely nothing was going on there. Most of the staff would be gone, a few of us crazies would have just moved on to greener pastures, and the whole place would be dead quiet. You can only read so much Chekhov before the silence drives you mad.

In the end, I faced one final meeting with a career army officer. It was scary because the guy was stern and sat as straight as a ramrod, and I felt like he was looking right through my game. We had a very interesting little discussion. Everything was on the edge of a knife.

The guy was glancing through my records. He said, "So, you want to get out of the army, huh?" He smiled.

"Yeah, that would be nice." At the same time, I thought, "Oh shit, he's got me figured out."

He was looking straight through me. "Because you just can't take it anymore, right?"

"Yes."

"I see."

I was shaking to my roots, but none of it mattered to him. He smiled again and just said, "Okay, then you're done. You can go home. Sign here. Have a good time."

And just like that, I was out. Which meant I had to go home to my parents again. I don't think they were expecting much from me in the army. They just weren't expecting me home so soon.

\*　　　\*　　　\*

After coming out of the army, I had a few months left before going back to acting school. There was all summer. After getting my head straight, I decided to go on a holiday to Switzerland and climb mountains. They have quite a collection there. All shapes and sizes. I rode the five hundred miles down from Holland on my motorcycle.

I had a classic BMW 600 and got there in one piece, although I had a scary moment zigzagging up one of the Alps passes. It had started to get foggy as the altitude climbed. Right at the top of the crossing, temperatures were really freezing, and as the road started to slowly bend downward and curve to the left, I noticed the ice that covered the cobblestones and I realized I would not be able to make the curve. On the right-hand side, the shoulder of the road was leaping off into the valley. I jumped off the bike. It was a simple move which saved my life and made me realize how lucky I'd always been.

I think I did that for a week and then started looking for a summer job. I had some contacts in a village called Dornach. Since I had done quite a few jobs like set builder, painter, and stagehand, I was able to find a job at the Goetheanum, which is a massive theater there. At night I would be a stagehand on many productions, some of which would last several hours. There was one production which lasted for all of seven hours: *Das Leiden des Jungen Werthers*. I think it was by Schiller—shoot me if I am wrong.

At the same time, I found I could be a gardener during the day as well. After a week or so I found a house which I could share with a British painter and a young German man. We lived there together for a few months. Each would disappear sometimes as well. I remember the German and the Brit would have these great conversations—the Brit not having a clue about German and the German having *keine ahnung* for English. But they would talk. With patience and some form of understanding. Who knows?

I was spending time on the bike and would climb onto a tall rock at sunset and read Nietzsche. So darn interesting—sharp and grim. There was an incredible coffee, tea, and cake house in this village, and we met some Swiss girls there. They invited us to come visit them in the guesthouse of some uncle. It was all sudden, brief, and stormy. It took us a week to explore, then her parents called the police and the girl I had just met and fallen in love with disappeared out of my life. I had no idea where she lived or any address for her.

The summer went by in seconds. I went back to Amsterdam and acting school. And I studied. This time I would climb through the four years of daytime school with occasional problems but eventually I would finish it. Meanwhile, I had tracked down the Swiss girl, and a year later I rode down to Lugano in the south of Switzerland and got a job as a waiter to support myself while I would stalk the house where she lived with her parents.

I was there for a few weeks. Saw her once, not knowing it would be just that once. I went out gambling one night with a few other guys and lost all my wages. So I had to work two more weeks to make the money for the trip back.

In my third year of school she visited Amsterdam and spent one night at my small room in the middle of the city. How to describe the room? It was on the first floor in a very ancient brick building along a canal. The stairs were on such a steep angle that it was hard not to hit your knees on them while walking up. The wooden floor of the two-window room was ten feet wide and forty feet long and it was slanted—it was a room on a tilt. It was poor and artistic.

By the end of that year it turned out she was pregnant. I had no intention of marrying. Nor was I ready for babies. She said she went for an abortion, which was difficult then. She was lying. The next year she lived in Switzerland and gave birth to a daughter. I was still in school, but when the baby was two months old I went there in a small borrowed car. The mess I found daughter and mother in made me feel I had to show responsibility. I loaded both of them into the car and took them back with me to a small farm in which I then lived, and we married. Three months later, we moved onto a barge which was moored in Amsterdam. I planned to turn its cargo hold into a nice home.

It wouldn't be that way. One night my new wife, with baby in her arms, and my sister got into an argument. I was not sure what it was about. I just stood there until my wife dropped the baby in order to hit my sister. My reflexes were quick enough to catch her. The baby was three months old, mind you.

The world changed. I moved out. My wife disappeared without leaving an address or number. I sold the barge and went back to school. Eventually, I divorced. The mother raised the daughter. So I did not have a crazy wife anymore. The daughter gave me a grandson. I am proud of how they took the hurdles and built their own lives. I carry them with me in my heart, and see them when I can.

In 1967, I graduated from school after three years and got offered an acting job with the Noorder Compagnie. If I took the job, I'd have to leave the city behind and move by myself into the country where the roads were narrow and very little was happening. It would be a big change, but one I thought I might like. I was never really a city guy anyway—the famous Amsterdam nightlife was wasted on me. Occasionally, I might go out to a club, jump on the dance floor, and dance the night away. But I only went out once in a while and I didn't really do the party scene. I was fencing, and doing some ballet, and going to the theater at night. There was a lot of avant-garde theater coming to Amsterdam, and there were also plays from America. I studied and worked hard in that period. I wanted to succeed . . . at something.

The Noorder Compagnie was a good way to get working. It was a nice company. It was small. And they had an attractive idea—to bring the theater to the farmers rather than have the farmers come to the Palace of the Arts.

# CHAPTER 5

## THE START OF SOMETHING LOVELY

One night, I was doing a poetry reading at a café in a small village. While I was with the theater, I would do poetry readings on the side—out loud and in public. I even used to read some of my own poetry. After this particular reading, I was getting ready to leave and it was starting to snow. It had been a late evening, and when I got outside, my car, an old red Porsche, refused to start. I was stranded.

A guy from the reading came up to me. "What's the problem?"

"Well, the car doesn't want to start."

"Why don't you stay at our house and we'll take care of it tomorrow?"

It was late, and I didn't see any other choice. "Well, that's very nice. Okay, that's great. Thank you, I will." The guy's name was Marius.

I went home with him and he gave me his own bed while he slept in the living room. The next morning, when I woke up, I got breakfast in bed, served by his mother, who was quite a beautiful woman. I'd never had breakfast in bed before. The bed was snug, the eggs were delicious, and the morning light broke softly through the window. I lay back, contented and at ease. I had come in late at night, I was a total stranger, and yet they were treating me so kindly.

After I ate, I got dressed and I walked into the living room. I remember feeling right at home there. Then I met Marius's sister. Her name was Ineke. She was beautiful, charming, and witty. And I thought, "How interesting."

She said, "I'm going to the beach. Do you want to come?" She told me there was a place next to the sea where she would make collages out of whatever waste would wash up there. I said, "Sure, that'll be fun."

My car was dead, so we took her car—a funny little Citroën Deux Chevaux, a tiny French car, the most economical of cars. It had two cylinders and two horsepower. It was like a duck on the road—the Dutch would call it the Ugly Duck. It had trouble with headwind. She couldn't get it into fourth gear because the wind was too strong. But we drove to the sea and we had a great time together. I sat back on a mound and watched her collect her materials. Sometimes we would talk—just little bits of conversation. We could be quiet together without being awkward.

Ineke says she knew that I was the one for her that first day by the sea. I had no idea, but I really liked her, and we stayed in contact. What's most interesting about it—what gives it a sense of destiny—is that we had actually met before.

More than a year earlier, I was driving in the northern countryside after I had accepted the job with the Noorder Compagnie. I was driving my Porsche on a very empty country road, enjoying the scenery. Somebody approached me from the opposite direction. It was a tiny car—a Deux Chevaux. It passed me, and when it did, the driver honked on the horn a couple of times. I caught a flash of blond hair and the wave of a hand. I thought, "Uh-oh. I might be losing the exhaust or something." I stopped the car and looked underneath, but nothing was wrong. "What the hell?" I didn't know what had happened, and the other car was long gone.

The second time, in late 1968, I was living on my own at my tiny rented farm, acting with the theater. I had been there only a short time. There was a yearly party, a book-release party where they would show off all the books that were coming out the next year. It was held in the theater where we worked. I went to this party just to see what it was all about and dance my socks off.

There was a band playing and I danced for a moment with this beautiful young woman that I met there. We danced for maybe two minutes, and what really struck me was her lovely white dress, very distinctive, which she told me she had made herself. I said, "What are you doing later?" And she said, "Well, we're going to this big party at this other place. It should be fun. You should meet us there."

After the song was over, I went to get my stuff, and when I came out, she had disappeared on me. But I remembered what she had said. The place that she mentioned was a café about thirty or forty miles up north. I drove there, and when I arrived, the door was locked, the lights were out, and the chairs were up on tables. She had pulled my leg, and now I had pretty much lost her. I didn't even know her name.

Of course, when Marius brought me home with him that first time, I didn't immediately connect Ineke with these earlier incidents. But one day much later I noticed the same white dress in her closet—one of her passions was designing and making dresses. She went to a school specifically for clothing design. I said, "This dress. I've seen this dress before. I think it was at this book party. I danced with this girl, and she left. She said she was going to another party. I followed her a long way, and when I got there, she had lied to me. Do you think that was you?"

She smiled. "It's possible because my dad is the editor of the newspaper that sponsors the party. So maybe it was me. I was there very briefly."

And I said, "Well, I'm sure it was you."

"And that red Porsche of yours," she said. "I've seen that before."

Then she told me a story about how more than a year earlier, she was driving in the country and enjoying the views when she saw a red Porsche, going slow. She thought, "Hey, I like that car, and I wonder who the blond guy was driving it." She honked as she passed him. *Beep, beep.* But then the guy stopped his car, climbed out, and looked under it, like something was wrong. Silly guy. She was only trying to flirt with him.

It wasn't long before Ineke and I were living together, and I became one of her family. Marius grew to be a dear friend, and so did Ineke's parents. We were all there together the night *Floris* first aired.

What happened when it hit the screen was beyond what I expected. It was beyond what the director Paul Verhoeven, or the writer Gerard Soeteman, or the other actors, or the producers, or anyone associated with this show expected. *Floris* very quickly became the most-watched program in Dutch television history.

As the lead character on the show, I became an instant TV star at age twenty-five, and was widely recognized throughout the country. Which isn't to say that I became rich. There was very little money involved in the making of *Floris*.

However, the show did have a nice effect on the Noorder Compagnie. In the years following *Floris*, we became more popular than ever. When we played a town, you could bet the theater would be packed—people from miles around came to see the clown from the TV show do his little dance in person. That was great fun—it gave the shows an added boost, a wink and a nudge, and a spark beyond what we were doing in the script. I played to that as much as I could, and enjoyed myself on the stage more than I had before.

We were welcome entertainers. We gave them as much quality as we could, and they gave us the best thing any audience can give a theater company—like children, they opened their minds to what we were doing and allowed themselves to believe in it and go for the ride with us.

One of the really exciting moments for me was when an American, Peter Feldman, came to work with us. Peter was one of two directors of the Open Theater in New York City, which was a very special, avant-garde theater. Our artistic director invited him to come over and direct *Of Mice and Men* by John Steinbeck and he and I had an immediate, strong connection. The link between us was right there because my English was pretty good. So just in terms of language I was way ahead of everybody. I translated the play into Dutch.

All the while, Ineke and I were together, living in our little rustic farmhouse. We farmed our own vegetable plot. We pumped our own water. I had tasted success, and maybe it was leading somewhere. We were together, we were in love, and things were good.

# CHAPTER 6

## TURKISH DELIGHT

It was the hottest film project in Holland.

In 1972, many of the same people who had created *Floris* were beginning production on a full-length feature film called *Turkish Delight*.

*Turkish Delight* is the story of Erik, a passionate young artist, who meets a beautiful young woman named Olga. The two free spirits embark on a wild love affair, until Olga's increasingly erratic actions end the relationship. Later, Erik learns that Olga's behavior was caused by a brain tumor which will kill her. He returns to her, and stays alone by her side until the end. A sweet turkish delight is his final gift to her.

The screenplay was based on the novel of the same name by Dutch author and sculptor Jan Wolkers. Taking place in

1958, *Turkish Delight* was both the most controversial, and the most beloved, novel in Dutch history. It is still the most successful bestseller ever published in the Netherlands—in four years it had thirty reprints and sold three hundred thousand copies. At first, it was put on the reading list for high school students. It was a great book, but it also appealed to the kids because the graphic sex in the story made it so naughty. As a result, it was soon banned from the list. Holland being such a liberal country, this had rarely happened before. And the controversy played right into the hands of the film.

When word got out that Paul Verhoeven had in mind to make this story into a movie, there was considerable gossip about the production before it even started. Even though time had passed since the making of *Floris*, there was still not much of a film industry in Holland. Verhoeven had made one feature film between *Floris* and *Turkish Delight*—a movie called *Business Is Business*, a sort of comedy about prostitutes, which was plagued by financial trouble and which was a big success as well.

As soon as I heard about *Turkish Delight*, I wanted to be in it. For one, I loved the novel and I loved the writer Jan Wolkers. His was one of the first books after *Lady Chatterely's Lover* that really addressed the questions of sex and love and loss in a way that felt natural, but was unconventional. For another, I felt that I understood the material deeply. I had been living a love story with Ineke for more than three years now—for the first time, I knew what love was, I felt it very deeply, and I wanted to tell that story.

Paul never even invited me to do a screen test. Paul never

does the obvious. Every project he works on, he tries to find new and interesting talent. So I called someone working for him and said I'd be more than willing to come in and do a screen test if he would let me. They said okay, but I wasn't at all certain I would get the part. In the end, when I did my test, Paul just felt that it seemed so natural and came so easy that he started to really see the role for me.

Much was made about the nudity in this film. I spend a fair amount of screen time in the nude, and I do full frontal nudity, something you rarely see in a mainstream movie in the United States. My costar, Monique Van de Ven, who was nineteen years old at the time, is also nude in much of the movie, and does full nudity. A handful of other actresses, perhaps three or four, spend some screen time in the nude and have lovemaking scenes.

Movie fans always seem interested in knowing about these types of scenes. Is something going on there? There's nothing intimate or romantic about it. First of all, fifty-nine crew members are walking around, getting things ready, and they're taking forever, seventeen hours a day with hot lights on you the whole time and you're sweating profusely before you ever make the first move.

The most fun I ever had doing a love scene came years later, after I had started my international career. It was a film called *Eureka*, directed by Nicolas Roeg, which we filmed in Jamaica.

I had a scene with Theresa Russell. In the film, Gene Hackman played her father and was supposed to catch us making love. It was shot in one of those nice huts on the water, just beautiful surroundings. We were supposed to do three or four lines, on a pillow together, sort of hanging out after sex. Then Dad walks into the room. "What the hell are you doing?"

We were just finishing the scene with a closer shot of Theresa and me lying on the pillow. As we got ready to shoot, we discovered there was a fly. It wasn't a big deal. But Theresa and I were lying there and—from the corner of my eye I saw it sitting there. The moment we rolled camera and we started doing our scene, the fly landed on the middle of the pillow right between our heads.

"Okay, cut! Let's get that fly out of there. All right, let's go again." They chased the fly away and we started again. But the same thing happened—the fly dropped into the shot and sat somewhere else, and a love scene with a fly just isn't very romantic. Now everybody was kind of giggling, and Nicolas was going "Well, can somebody get the fly out of the room so we can work?"

People tried to hit the fly, and the fly went away somewhere. We start shooting again. This time the fly didn't show up, but now there was a big dog outside the hut, somewhere nearby, and it started barking. *Woof, woof, woof.* So somebody went out and quieted the dog. Ready again. But then there was an engine revving outside, and that screwed us up. By now it's take five, and as we're going for the take, here comes the fly again. He landed on the pillow.

Now everybody was getting a bit nervous. Delays cost a lot of money in moviemaking. Nicolas said, "We gotta do something about this fly. So let's take a break."

They sent people to find a can of some nasty chemical, like

DDT. That wasn't readily available on the set—they had to go to a shop to actually buy a spray can. That took them half an hour, then they came back and sprayed the whole place. So now we were ready—we had to move into this room that was full of poison and do our love scene. We should have been wearing gas masks. We're now on take six or seven. We start the take, and there's the fly again. It's an atomic fly—the chemicals don't bother it. It took us three hours to get that one shot, upstaged by a fly the whole time.

Of course, in *Turkish Delight*, the nudity and sex were not the only things to focus on—this was a graphic film in every way. The hardest thing for me was that my character had a sadistic streak. There were some brutal moments. I had to be blunt and raw, and treat the women like sex objects, using them and discarding them, all because it was in the script. I hated those moments. And there were moments where I had to be cruel to Olga's mother, especially one where I punch her on her fake breast—she had breast cancer and had had the breast removed. I had a hard time with it.

As part of my preparation for the role, I got to spend time with Jan Wolkers. I had some good talks with him, and he gave me a sculpture lesson at his studio, just to give me a feel of how it was done. It was exciting to see what the real person was like as opposed to the writer. He was a warm and friendly person. I still felt his passion, but I could talk to the man and we could understand each other.

Outside of the occasional bits of cruelty, the difference between the character and me wasn't very big. Erik Vonk was just a guy like me, an artist. I would bring certain things that were from my own life. There are a couple of moments in the movie where Wolkers later said, "You nailed it." That's the best compliment you can get, and those were not in the book. They came from making the movie and they came from me.

We shot quickly, in about six weeks. We did very little rehearsing, and everything was done in a few takes. We didn't have enough money to do a lot of takes. That was the story in those days—there was no money for anything. Everything was shot on location—in homes, on the beach, on the streets of Amsterdam.

In those days, Paul knew good acting when he saw it. He had a great eye for what was believable. He just didn't know how to get there. His take on acting and how to do it was mostly "Don't indulge yourself if you can help it. Don't show me the acting."

I remember moments in the shoot when Paul and I were really close. I would come to do a scene and I would say to him, "You know, I'm not ready for this. I don't know what this scene is about. I don't know what you want here." And he would look at me for a moment and say, "I don't either. But we have to shoot this scene now, we're way behind schedule, so let's, eh, let's just try to do something."

The cinematographer on the film was Jan de Bont, who had also worked on *Floris*, and who would work on many films with Paul Verhoeven, up to and including *Basic Instinct*. Later, de Bont became a director in his own right, and directed the hit film *Speed*, with Keanu Reeves. De Bont suggested that they shoot everything in *Turkish Delight* with handheld cameras. He felt that handheld cameras, rather than stationary cameras, would provide more intimacy, and more movement, which was ideal for a film like this. And Verhoeven agreed. He felt the handheld cameras gave enormous freedom for improv acting. At times, Paul would explain what emotion he wanted, within the context of the script, and then let the actors go.

When the film came out, people were blown away. If *Floris* had been an explosion, then *Turkish Delight* was like the atomic bomb going off. In Holland, it was hugely popular and controversial. It was by far the most-talked-about film of the year, and it became the country's most popular and beloved film—a position it holds to this day. And for the first time, a Dutch film made a real impact outside of Holland.

*Turkish Delight* was a hit all over Europe, even with subtitles. This was something beyond understanding. In Holland, we were used to importing films and watching them with subtitles—it never happened that we would export a film. But *Turkish Delight* was different. In Berlin, in France, in England— all over Europe they were watching it. In Italy, it played longer than *Love Story* and *Cabaret,* and even Marlon Brando's *Last Tango in Paris.*

Now I was a movie star, and so was Monique. It was a beautiful, surreal experience. I was still on the farm. The phone was not ringing off the hook with people wanting to talk to me about my great success—Ineke and I didn't even have a phone yet. I didn't make that much money—about six thousand guilders, which would be about $2,500 for the whole movie.

The film was just out there, running in theaters for a long time. And after they packed everything up, there still wasn't a film industry in Holland. I couldn't even be certain that I'd ever make another film. I just thought it was a beautiful script, a beautiful opportunity, and I was happy to do it. That it would capture a huge international audience never occurred to me.

In 1999, *Turkish Delight* was voted Best Picture of the Century by the people of the Netherlands. On the same occasion, I was given the Best Actor of the Twentieth Century award in the Netherlands, and was celebrated on Dutch television with a compilation of my films. A few years earlier, in 1995, the Dutch Mail Service issued a stamp with Monique and I doing a scene from *Turkish Delight*. That this film still moves people in Holland so long after we made it is most gratifying.

The only disappointment was that my parents never saw the film. Much like Paul Verhoeven's father, they were mortified by the whole thing. They said, "We don't read that sort of book." So they didn't look at the movie. My parents were liberal people for their times, but they were traditional in their own way. They didn't like movies with guns, and they didn't like movies with sex. In their minds you didn't talk about sex, and you certainly didn't make a movie about it, so they couldn't bring themselves to bear it for me.

\*         \*         \*

After all of the hubbub died down, I was still with the Noorder Compagnie, and still made most of my modest living on the stage. It was right back to work, but things had begun changing with the theater company, and not for the better.

There was a new artistic director and I had a bad feeling about him. He was a macho guy, and he was a power freak. He also had some film experience, but not in Holland—he came from Yugoslavia. He had decided he was going to be the boss of the company. And I didn't accept him as the boss—I accepted him as an artistic leader, but not as the boss. In fact, they had offered me the job first, and had asked me to step into that role. The original artistic director had a health problem. So they needed somebody else, but it was too much for me. I wasn't ready. It scared me—there was too much of a commitment to something that I wasn't quite sure about it.

It all came to a head a short time after *Turkish Delight*. At some point, I had invented a Friday, Saturday, and Sunday series of short one-act plays. I was developing and directing them. Then the new artistic director came to me and said that he didn't want me running these plays. He shut me down. It was an odd and painful thing to have happen. Certainly, he may have envied my success a little. But I think his very presence was a symptom of a larger problem—the theater company was suffering from its own success.

The whole story of the theater and acting has been that actors were travelers and vagabonds, going from town to town. But then they stopped traveling and theater started to become the temple of the arts, and things started to change. To me that change always felt like something was lost, some connection with the audience, and the actors went Hollywood on themselves. So the whole idea of traveling to where farmers lived and worked to do plays was very interesting. I had been really curious to see if that would work, and when it did, I was as excited as anybody by our success.

The thing that was rotten in the middle was how that success spoiled the fruit, and the coming of this artistic director heralded that things had completely changed. It basically came down to the same old song. In five years' time they turned from wanting to go to the farmers to wanting to make the farmers come to the theater. So the company itself turned around on its initial goals. I felt sad about that but there was nothing I could do to prevent it.

I saw that this was in progress and I saw it develop into this bourgeois theater. And then the new boss came in and said he didn't want me directing my series of plays. Coupled with the other changes under way, I saw disaster looming. I confronted him on it and he said, "Well, if you can't work with me the way I want, you better go." So I fired myself. Just like that. I didn't have anything on the horizon at that moment, and I didn't have much money. I was sort of casting myself into the unknown, but it didn't take me twenty seconds to decide. I just said, "Okay, I'm out of here."

It was a fateful decision, but I had no way of knowing that. I went home, and after a couple of days, with no prospects, I signed up to go on welfare.

# CHAPTER 7

## THE *MAX HAVELAAR* INCIDENT

I was on welfare for two weeks.

It was a load off my mind to escape from that. In Holland, we value the ideal of taking care of everyone whether they can work or not. Even so, I wanted to work. If society would not stigmatize me for being out of work, I am a proud man and I felt the stigma within myself. Would it be possible to make a living as a film actor? That was the question. It turned out there was no reason to worry.

*Turkish Delight* was my stamped ticket into the film industry, and soon I was working again. The offers came, and that year, I did three more films. I was still living on the farm in the country. That was my base. A tiny little farm next to a small river—very beautiful, and very much away from everything. And finally we had a phone line installed.

Within a short period of time, I did a German thriller called *Cold Blood*, and then I did a German film called *Pusteblume*, which in English means "Dandelion." It was also known as, in one of the more amusing titles of my career, *De Blonde Love-Machine*. Basically a copycat of *Turkish Delight*, the movie follows the exploits of Erik, who wastes his life with lots of women, motorcycle rides, and alcohol while completely obsessed by a poster of a girl blowing on a dandelion. I was making a living, and enjoying it, but the films I was doing could have been better.

Around that time, I did a German TV series, shot in Hungary, called *Floris von Rosemund*. This was a partial remake of the original *Floris* show that had created my first success in Holland—except we added a bunch of new episodes to some of the earlier ones. It was shot in German and came with an avant-garde Austrian director named Ferry Radax. He was a horseman and an intellectual. He loved poetry—a filmmaker to the bone.

We had a great time together, with tremendous shared silliness and the longest discussions about everything—art and life and the dark side of the moon. We had an incredible bond. We both had blooded horses to ride. Each morning, the Hungarian stuntmen would invite us to warm up from the cold and join them in a first plum drink—called *paratz*—which tended to have enough alcohol in it to sink a submarine. I don't hold my liquor well, so I had to decline their manly offer while they drank the courage to throw themselves off the walls of the castles—which they did with pride, great expertise, and big smiles.

The other jolly experience I had during this shoot was

dealing with the Hungarian language. Very few of the crew spoke English—none really. Some spoke sporadic German, or a little Russian. Misunderstandings were normal and took time to be resolved. On a few occasions we had Hungarian actors playing small parts in the show. They did the Hungarian/German version of how Inspector Clouseau would speak English—sometimes the way they pronounced the German was so bad, it was pretty much useless. So then they would do their lines in Hungarian. It became a sport to figure out what they would say, and in what language. I would wait wide-eyed for the verbal Hungarian rhapsody to pause, and then I would respond with my lines. It was both scary and hilarious. I remember it fondly.

I was having a German career there for a moment. Although the *Floris* remake was successful in Germany, I decided to improve in terms of what projects I would take on. If only I could figure out how.

One interesting project that came to me around that time was a supporting role in an English-language film called *The Wilby Conspiracy*. This film starred the great American actor Sidney Poitier as the South African revolutionary leader Shack Twala, opposite the great British actor Michael Caine. It was a thriller, and kind of a buddy movie, with these two on the run from the forces of apartheid in South Africa. I spent two months in Kenya making this film, another new and eye-opening experience for me in the business.

This was my first major English-language film. The size of the production was mind-boggling. I couldn't believe it. We spent much of our time out in the Kenyan desert. The vistas were startling, beautiful, unearthly, and we were like a small army encampment—so many people, so much machinery, vehicles, tools. I hadn't seen anything like that before. The biggest movie I remember making before that cost about five million guilders, which was about two and a half million dollars. We had worked with crews of maybe fifty people—at the most. *The Wilby Conspiracy* shoot had three times that many people and many who had traveled halfway around the world to get there. It was almost like working at a factory, in the sense that there are all these people around that you will never get to know.

Also, for the first time, I found it hard to be away from home. We take good phone links for granted nowadays, but communications from Kenya to Europe in the mid–1970s left a lot to be desired. In Kenya, you had to dial through an operator whose English would be flawed. Sometimes their abilities would also be flawed. They'd say that they would call back, and they wouldn't. Or the circuits would be busy. Or the line would work but you had to shout. Or there would be these weird echoes on the line, making it impossible to understand what anyone was saying.

Things got so bad with the phones that we had to hit upon a different solution. My father-in-law was the editor of the *Friesche Koerier*, a small Dutch newspaper. He had a telex at home. I gave up on the frustrating attempts to call and would communicate through the telex machine at my hotel. I would bribe the hotel personnel, depending on who was on duty, and they would let me sit there in the late-night hours. Ineke was on the other side, and we took turns typing out messages. Even then, I couldn't do it too often and the bribes didn't always work.

Although it was tough, it was also a big opportunity. It was the first time I worked with international stars like Poitier and Caine. It was a little breathtaking to be around them, but there was nothing to worry about. They were both friendly to me, and Michael was always cracking jokes and making everyone laugh. I played a bad guy. It was a small role, but I did have a scene with Sidney Poitier. We did a fight scene together, and the funny thing was, he was a lot bigger than I imagined. I remember him as being a head taller than me.

When we tussled, I found out something else about him—he was strong. I remember thinking, "Whoa! Wait a minute here." It was a simple wrestling match, and the power he put into it was more than I expected. I tend to put very little power in my moves. But if somebody starts putting power into anything, you have to come up with more power to work it your way—and then it starts to become real.

Within a couple of minutes, the battle was on. Some friendly testosterone flowed, we pushed, we pulled, the heavy breathing came—I couldn't move him, and he couldn't move me. In the film, he's the hero and he kicks my ass. In real life, call it a tie, and we were both laughing like two young boys by the end.

"Hey, Rutger, you're a hell of a strong guy," he said when we were done.

"Well, if you start pushing me around, I have to do something."

"Yeah," he said. "It's true."

Sidney's film work had been revolutionary in terms of challenging racial stereotypes and the status quo, and he was a megastar at that time, even in Kenya. In fact, he was revered in

Kenya, and he was invited to meet the president of the country while we were filming. Sidney was not just a star—he was a symbol, and he carried a lot of responsibility on his back. Yet he seemed to carry that load lightly, and he gave of himself to people in a big way.

After we finished our scene, a group of people had gathered to meet him and get his autograph. This must have been a daily event for him. He took it in stride, treating everyone with a certain sweetness that you don't always see in this business. I don't mean that he was just kind to people. I mean he took all the time needed to talk to every individual, and he joked or played around with each one. Watching him work and play was a treat.

I saw him recently, for the first time in the nearly three decades since we made *The Wilby Conspiracy*. I was in Vancouver, shooting two episodes for the TV show *Smallville*. I was riding down the escalator in a local shopping mall. I heard a voice. "Hi, Rutger! How have you been and how are you doing?" I looked down and saw him riding the escalator up. I waved as we passed. "I'm good. May even direct something. Nice seeing you here!" Just before he reached the top, he yelled, "Put me on your list. I'll give you a very nice price!" Thank you, Sidney.

I waited in Kenya for almost two months before finally filming my scenes. Since I had all that time on my hands, and since I had to play a pilot, they hooked me up with a small airplane charter company to get some idea of what I was supposed to be doing as the character. I had always wanted to learn how to fly, but had neither the time nor the money. So they showed me some of the ropes while on the ground and took me for a few loops. It was quickly decided that I had a definite hand for it.

One day, I flew to Nairobi, the capital city of Kenya. From the air, I got to see the sights of the different wild animals, as well as the villages of the Maasai tribespeople. On the ground in Nairobi, I saw the city's shopping center—where the last ivory and skins were being traded to silly tourists in clean new safari outfits.

Back in Holland, I found an agent, and he eventually started getting me work in more films. I was making a living as an international film actor in German and English. In just a few years I had done perhaps ten pieces of work, some of which were wonderful and enjoyed enormous success. I was frolicking through life with a passion.

It was 1975 by now, and I was cast in the lead role for *Max Havelaar*, a film that was going to be shot on location in Indonesia for two months. It was the true-life story of Max Havelaar, a colonial administrator who struggled against the status quo of imperialism imposed by the Dutch people in their Indonesian colonies during the 1800s. In the story, as in history, Max was a strong man who got dragged into mortal combat with the system. It was a beautiful part, with some great stuff about this guy standing up to the worst aspects of colonialism. This was a lead role and I was looking forward to the shoot. We were all set.

Just before the twelve-hour flight to Indonesia, I got a call from my agent. The film company was backing out of the deal. They no longer wanted me to play Max Havelaar. How about a secondary role instead? They had given the part to another actor. Good for him, but I had signed a contract. "Sue them," I said. "They can't do this."

My agent suggested that suing them might not be a good idea. "I know this hurts," he said, "but it's two months in Indonesia anyway. It's another movie. You get a trip around the world. It's not ideal, but it's not that bad. And I'll get you some good money."

I wasn't crazy about it. For the first time, I was facing a compromise. Inside me, alarm bells were going off. "Just say no. Something else will come along." To this day, I still think we could have sued. There just weren't a whole lot of people around in those days who knew how that worked. My agent either didn't know how to do it, or maybe he didn't want to fight for me. I didn't want to do it, but I agreed anyway. I swallowed hard, packed my suitcase, and went. Ineke would follow me later.

We shot for about a month while I was alone in Indonesia. We filmed in the jungle, three or four hours outside of Jakarta, the major city. The locations were authentic—including the very house where Havelaar was stationed a century before. The jungle itself seemed a menacing presence—it was hot and dense and intriguing. The lighting drove the director of photography crazy. "All that green," he would say. "NOTHING BUT GREEN!"

The pace of work was slow and we had to wait long hours and days to get shots set up. Even so, I wasn't exactly an unhappy camper. I had a cottage on the beach. The surf was huge, and loud. The sunsets were millions of colors, and even the thunder from coconuts dropping on the metal roof at night wasn't a bad thing. *Bonk! Bonk!* Soothing, like the world's most gigantic raindrops. During my many off-hours, I read. I swam. I joined the family members of the rest of the cast in games on the beach, or helped the babysitter Judith watch the cast members' offspring. The little ones were a wild bunch and kept me busy. It was an easygoing, lighthearted time. I began to think that my agent had been right after all. The day before Ineke came to join me, I went to the market and got her tons of little presents. I was ecstatic in anticipation of being together in this paradise. The next afternoon, I headed into the city to pick her up.

Driving in Indonesia was a nightmare. Real taxis were hardly available—people crammed into death-trap minibuses. The roads were narrow, one lane in each direction. Cars would pass anyway, sometimes jamming themselves right down the center of the road. At night the cars would only have their parking lights on, driving along roads full of cows, dogs, and people carrying baskets on their heads. That's what the trip was like from the set to the airport.

I made a reservation to have dinner in a very nice hotel where we would spend the night, then move to the cottage the next day. I picked her up at the airport after her long flight. We snoozed a few hours, and around midnight, we went for supper. I had told the maître d' our menu ahead of time, and we were all on our own in the beautiful hotel restaurant. The waiters were gentle and sweet, and between each course I brought out little gifts. We had a ball, eating and unwrapping presents for three hours.

The next morning, in a real taxi, we left at ten-thirty, planning to head to the set, maybe have lunch there, and then drive on to the coast. The road through the countryside had some very narrow spots with tall eucalyptus trees on both sides. Drivers would pass each other from time to time, veering out into the lane of oncoming traffic. Ineke was dozing beside me and I was watching through the window. Both of us were in the backseat.

It happened in three seconds. Traveling in the opposite direction, one car overtook another. Our driver hit his brakes, but there was nowhere to go. The cars slammed into each other, a head-on collision. The noise was incredible. At the last second, I tried to hold Ineke, but the force of impact was too much. She was thrown forward. Her face and her body crashed into the chair in front of her.

Everything went silent and I was sure she was dead.

Then the screaming started. The next thing I knew, we were outside the car, on the side of the road. The taxi was a wreck, the driver bleeding in his seat. Ineke and I were on the ground, and I cradled her in my arms. Her face was cut open and bleeding from exploded glass. Was she alive? Was she dead? A tooth fell into my hand and she started to moan. Hundreds of people were gathering, cars were blowing horns, people were yelling. I didn't understand the language. We were in a very strange land, and very far from home.

I thought: "This is my woman. Please let her live."

Some people helped us onto the flatbed of a truck, and it raced us to a nearby hospital. On the ride, all the way, I kept repeating to her: "I will never leave you." When we arrived at the hospital the first thing I saw after opening the door were a bunch of dirty curtains, and a bloody bucket in one corner with what looked like an amputated leg in it. A horror movie couldn't do better. Ineke was moaning in pain, and the doctor came out with an enormous needle. It could have been for a horse. My God! I stood in front of her, fending him off. "What is it for?" His English was minimal. It was a tetanus shot, but it took him some time to make me understand this.

It turned out that her injuries were bad, but thankfully not life-threatening. She had a concussion and she'd broken her wrist. Her wrist and arm had to be reset and put in a cast. Later, back home, X-rays would show that it could have been done better. The cuts she had all over were stitched up. Her torn lip was the hardest part. No anesthesia was available. Everything that was done could have been done better. It took years of work to repair the damage to her teeth.

Since she couldn't be moved for ten days, we were given a room in a new wing at the kids' section of the hospital. The wing was not yet occupied—it was empty except for us. The beds were brand-new, and the mattresses—designed for children—were too short. The new air-conditioning was not working yet and so the room was hot and humid. The sound of crying children came to us from other parts of the children's section, never letting up, not even at night.

Since light was painful for Ineke, I made makeshift blinds out of old clothes, sheets, and curtains. Every other day Judith, the babysitter I mentioned earlier, came to visit us with some news or magazines or fruit, and she would wash my wife.

The production company changed its schedule to accommodate me, so I didn't have to go to work right away. After ten days, we were able to move. I hired an ambulance and took Ineke "home" to the beach. With the kids there, some of my colleagues, and Judith, we were all right.

Even so, now, after all this time, I feel terrible about the experience. I had made a bad decision—we should not have been there in the first place. Movies are transient things. The production is over, and you go home. The movie comes out. Then the movie disappears and so does the money you made. The only things that stay are the trauma and the long years of work to recover. I should have followed my instinct. That knowledge is always with me.

One other thing is with me as well. After the accident, on our way to the hospital, as I held Ineke in my arms, a deep understanding got me. Yes, I had loved her before then. Yes, we had a good life together. In that extreme and terrible moment, it hit me solid as a rock: I felt the deepest and truest love for her. I would never leave her.

# CHAPTER 8

## SOLDIER OF ORANGE

A year can pass quickly.

After *Max Havelaar*, we went home to the country, and I took a break from acting. We had a little money now—more, at least, than we'd had in the past. I could afford a bit of time off. And there really wasn't much happening. Little did I know what was just around the corner.

I heard that Paul Verhoeven was casting for a film called *Soldier of Orange*, which would re-create the life and exploits of Erik Hazelhoff, a leader in the Dutch Resistance during World War II. Once again, I felt I should get at least a call from Paul, but the call never came. So I called him.

"I need to know," I said when he came on the line, "are you at all considering me for this role?"

A pause. "I don't think you can pull it off. Anyway, I'm looking for somebody new."

I deeply appreciated this. Once again, he was looking for a fresh, new talent for an important role. I applauded him for that, and still do. But I suggested to him that he give me a screen test if he had difficulty finding the right man. He said he would. That call came a month later.

When they sent the script, I hesitated myself. The project was ambitious, to say the least. It told the story of Erik, a hero of the Dutch Resistance, beginning with his pre-war student days as a wealthy young nobleman. When the Germans attack Holland, he tries to join the army, but the Dutch are defeated before he can even sign on. In occupied Holland, he and his friends gradually become more and more involved with the Resistance, until finally he is a wanted man and must flee the country. In England, he becomes a flyer for the Royal Air Force, and eventually returns to Holland victorious, and at the exiled Queen Wilhelmina's side. I read it several times and asked myself, "Is this really something I should do? Is it something I even *can* do?"

At that time, I hadn't heard of Erik Hazelhoff. He had written a book, but I hadn't read it. Regardless, I decided that I wanted the role. It was a dynamite script. As an actor, I felt it would make me stretch in ways I had never done before. I'm pretty sure that what got Paul when I did my screen test was that I had learned a few tricks over the years. We had filmed *Turkish Delight* four years earlier, but in those four years, I had done a lot of screen work. I was more confident and I felt more natural.

Erik Hazelhoff himself had some difficulty seeing me portray him. I think he was concerned because the first film in which I was successful had a lot of nudity in it, and that was not his cup of tea. Although we came from the same small country, there were some big gaps between us.

He went to university. His background was with royalty and writing, and my background was with actors and farmers, and growing up on the streets of Amsterdam. He was an intellectual from the higher classes, and I was . . . I don't know what you'd call it. I guess I've always felt closer to the workingman. My background didn't really bother him, but he had his doubts that I could play him, and so did I. I was not sure at all how I could pull it off, and if it would be believable. I would have to convince both of us along the way.

*Soldier of Orange* meant some of the bigger changes for me. First of all, the story itself changed my way of looking at things. The art of war had always been a mystery to me. Running around to kill someone because the higher-ranking guy just told you so—it's beyond my understanding. When I was in the army for a few months I was the fittest dog, but when it got serious I had to give up. I'm glad my country doesn't need me that way. And I'm pretty happy that I can just pretend to be a soldier as history keeps repeating this deadly game. I want no part of it.

Erik Hazelhoff became my guide in the miserable, deadly serious, and ridiculous adventure of war and Resistance. The interesting thing was that he felt the same way about war as I did. Nearly as much as me, he was a peace lover and something of a pacifist. The difference was that history and circumstances thrust him into this role of Resistance fighter. He never wanted to hurt anyone, and yet he loved his country so much that he felt he had no choice. He was the very definition of the reluctant hero.

Until this movie, I thought of my passes at film roles as a sport and a game. It came down to the idea "Can I make the viewer believe these characters and stories ring true?" By the time I was doing *Soldier of Orange* I had just succeeded in getting this semirealism down. So this was a screenplay I looked at with different eyes. I took a lot of time to decide how I wanted to play it. I approached the book, the screenplay, and the role with more thought and distance than any work before. I felt it was not close to home for me—I had never really been a soldier, and I had never been a hero, consistently risking my life for an idea. I felt it needed more acting skill. It certainly seemed like it needed a lot more work to make it mine.

My main concern was that it not be a war movie, with people's noble intentions all over the place. I wanted it to be as much about life as it was about everything else, including some humor amid the pain and suffering. I was hoping that there was a certain lightness to be captured, and maybe some silliness. I believe Erik has captured that in his books, and that's what I wanted. He talks about the stupidity and confusion in combat, and how all the human flaws are revealed when the pressure is on. My concern was I wanted to keep that—I wanted to keep all the bends and curves in, and not straighten them out.

Before shooting started, I did as much homework as I could, to get an idea of the time and the way people were. And of course because I had Erik as a source, it couldn't be better. I studied what he wrote. I studied his other books, and I let him guide me. I spoke to him several times, and when we were filming, he came to the set a few times—a tourist at his own life's story. And I started to get a feel for this character.

We shot much of the movie along the Dutch coast, and the shoot itself was demanding. Although this was the most expensive movie shoot in Dutch history, there were constant money troubles. When I look back at my diaries from that time, I see that Paul and producer Rob Houwer (whom he had teamed with several times before) were struggling the whole time to keep the thing afloat. At times, the lack of money had them at each other's throat. Here are a couple of diary entries from that autumn of 1977:

*October 15—Friday*

*Early this evening I discover my mostly kind director and mostly kind producer. From some distance. Their body language is troubled. Their voices low. Serious. "We're five days behind." That must be Producer Rob Houwer. Sighs. "You want me to stop shooting?" That's Paul Verhoeven, the director. Angry. What a job they have.*

*November 9—Tuesday*

*Paul V is furious. Our Producer has sent him another threat letter that we are way too far behind. It is nasty. The bad thing about it is that the letter has been copied and sent out into the crew. In the six weeks we've been shooting they have had three days off. The work hours have been very long. This is desperate, ugly, and bad. Discussions flare up among them. As tired as they are. The catering has been pretty bad. And it really looks more horrible today. I wish I could do something. Damn it. I*

*have 5 bucks on me. Next Paul V jumps in and invites
who is there to have dinner in a small restaurant. He
pays by cheque. 34 tournedos please. Grand. It eases
the tension somewhat. I'm pretty sure he won't ask the
producer to reimburse him. Paul is a good man.*

Paul Verhoeven is more than good—he is often amazing. He always gets it done and he goes through enormous strain to do it. Of course, I tried to help as much as I could, since we'd been together from the start—there was a team there, so he didn't have to hide too much. I always took the light road because I think a film shouldn't be able to kill you. As an actor, I tend to try not to let it eat into me too much. From their perspective, though, I can see how it was a lot of money and a lot of pressure.

Basically, weather and stunts are two major things that can cause money problems on a film set—and we had a lot of both while making this movie. They're risky elements, and sometimes take on a life of their own, causing endless delays. The conditions on *Soldier of Orange* were raw at times, and the situation would indeed get out of hand. I remember a night shoot that was one of the heaviest in my whole career. Night shoots are not easy to begin with. But this was one that took place in the ocean.

In the scene, Erik carries his friend and fellow Resistance fighter Guus (played by the great Dutch actor Jeroen Krabbé—probably best known in America for his role opposite Harrison Ford in *The Fugitive*) to the beach from a small British landing craft at sea. Guus is wearing a so-called dry diving suit with a tuxedo underneath. Erik carries him to keep him extra dry. After being dropped ashore, Guus takes off the dry suit and sneaks into Nazi-occupied Holland by pretending he is a guest at a formal party.

We spent the whole night in these dry suits. They were supposed to protect us and keep us dry, but they didn't work 100 percent. Instead, they had leaks and filled up with water. The surf was wild, and I had to carry Jeroen on my shoulders. I trudged through the waves while his supposedly watertight suit filled up, with sand as well as water. He weighed a ton. So I had all this weight on my shoulders while we did take after take, and the waves knocked us back and forth, and I tried to keep my balance. We finished shooting as the sun came up, and I still remember how tired I was as I collapsed into bed at 7 A.M. I could still feel the salt and smell the North Sea on my body. My thighs were like chewing gum and I was dead until four-thirty that afternoon.

Even less physically demanding scenes would get pretty funny sometimes. There was a scene where they dropped me in the ocean from this old British navy boat. The boat had to come past me—one of those dramatic shots—and I had to be picked up at end of that shot. We had rented this vintage British patrol boat left over from World War II. But the guys who owned it never mentioned that it had two forty-horsepower engines rather than the huge, thousand-horsepower engines it used to have. So the boat could do a top speed of about five knots. Now, in a good current and a good wind, five knots means that the boat does not go forward. It can only stay right where it is. Or it drifts sideways. So there I was, awash in heavy seas, half drowned, and the boat couldn't get to me because the wind and the current were too strong. It took us a while—thank God for great fins.

The special effects were crazy, too—especially the bombs. It's hard to explode a bomb that is in the water because you have to anchor the bomb, and in the ocean there's so much movement that things just don't stay where you put them. I remember that I had to go in the water—and it wasn't just me, we all had to run into the water as these bombs were going off—and afterward the special-effects guys had lost some equipment. They were looking for all this stuff. So I walked over to them.

"What are you looking for?"

"Well," they said, "we had big solid pieces of metal holding these bombs down and now they've disappeared." The bombs had gone off, now there were some very big pieces of metal missing, and luckily they didn't fall on anybody's head, thank you very much.

Special-effects people are all the same. They like things that go *boom*, and they always say, "No, don't worry. Everything's safe." But there's always a risk. That's what I've learned—as an actor, you have to keep the special-effects people away from you a little bit. Because here's the truth—everybody screws up once in a while, and so do they. The difference is, not everybody is playing with explosives when they screw up, and you don't want to be there when it happens. One time, on another film project, I was there.

We were in Hungary, in the countryside, shooting the second *Floris* series. The very last day of the shoot, they did an explosion, it was too big, and the horses went down. And these two stunt guys were on either side of me—one broke his neck, one broke his back, and I was in the middle of these guys. My horse went down, we rolled over, and through sheer luck I just got up and there was nothing wrong with me. I happened to walk away from it, but two stunt people were badly hurt and one of them never walked again. The other one had to wear a neck brace for a year.

In the end, we went to work on *Soldier of Orange* every day, not having a clue what it would mean for most of us down the line. It was a movie in Dutch. In that period "our" films would hardly have a chance of ever being seen across any border. *Turkish Delight* had been the one amazing exception—a love story with universal appeal. But *Soldier of Orange* was a very Dutch story—I didn't imagine for one minute that it would interest anyone outside the country. We thought that if we did it well, it would be a good film for Holland. And a subtitled release in America? Forget it. Americans don't like to read the movie.

The film premiered in Amsterdam in the fall of 1978, and we threw a big party that was attended by the royal family. This film was Dutch history, and a very big Dutch event. That night, I met the queen and the rest of the royal family. We shared a few awkward lines of conversation. I'm not a great conversationalist, so it was like "Hi. It's so nice to be here." And "How are you? I hope you like the movie."

When I finally saw the film, I knew we had something good. I was proud of the work I had done. The film itself was a very interesting document—a strange and funny movie, and a very nice movie from Paul Verhoeven—a movie with a beautiful human heart. Within a short time, we knew that audiences felt the same way. This movie ran and ran, crossing borders like wildfire, the way *Turkish Delight* had done.

There are moments that are really dear in the film. For instance, the sight of the Dutch Queen Wilhemina when she comes back from London after living in exile for five years and she steps off the Dakota 3 airplane. She rubs the sole of her shoe on the soil of the landing strip. But the scene that moves me the most is the last one.

In that scene, the war is over and Erik is having a toast with an old friend from the university. All of their other friends are dead. Erik has lived through one harrowing event after another. Meanwhile, his friend stayed in school, more or less ignored the war, and used his privileged station in life to isolate himself from the dangers. But now they are together again and still friends. I like the perspective and I've always liked it. It's that you can look back at a story with a different frame of mind—the victory is all around you, and was it really worth it? I know that Erik Hazelhoff had a very strong feeling about that, because it was in his writing and is in his person—he felt that part of all this is so silly. In the end, Erik's there with his friend who played no part in the fighting at all, and those two are the only ones who survived. And it's sort of like, "Well, cheers. Life goes on."

*Soldier of Orange* changed my life. It went big. It won the Los Angeles Film Critics Association Award as Best Foreign Film in 1979. It received a Golden Globe nomination as Best Foreign Film in 1980. And the fact that VHS videotape soon became a mainstream product, and TV networks started engulfing and absorbing worldwide airwaves with space that needed films, means that millions of people have seen this film at one time or another. It elevated this small and local story to another level, a place where it could reach the kind of audience that we would never expect. It launched our lives and careers. Paul Verhoeven, Jan de Bont, Derek de Lint, Jeroen Krabbé, and I were briefly lit by the limelight and all moved on from there.

Sometime after the film came out I was invited to the Egyptian Theater in Seattle, to the international film festival held there. At that time, there were two versions of *Soldier of Orange*. There was one that had been dubbed into English. It was a little shorter and it was action-oriented rather than character-oriented. Then there was the original version, which people had to follow by reading the subtitles. The two guys who owned the Egyptian fought to get the original version, and they showed it at their festival. They deserve a lot of credit for that because frankly, the easier, English-dubbed version was a half hour shorter and a bad film. So I went to the festival and ended up winning Best Actor. I saw how the American audience received the film—I never thought they would receive it so well. That attention built some interest, and helped to get a limited theater run going for the film in the United States.

A few months later, when the limited run was beginning, I came back to the United States, this time to do a press junket in New York City. I was there for a week, making one media appearance after another, talking to reporter after reporter after reporter. I had never done anything like that before. It was quite a shocking experience—high-pressure, intense, and a lot of work. I had a good press agent, who I was able to talk to. But I was a nervous wreck—it felt like I was going through twenty-nine different stomachs, with an ego attached to each one. And while I spoke English well, I had never before spoken so much English for so long. It is exhausting. It drains your brain. The way the people understand you, the way you understand them, the way all their interests are different from one another—every conversation is a new and curious adventure.

My press agent, who had been hired by the film company to handle me, was Nancy Selzer. She said, "Why don't you think of working in this country? You could do it. Your English is quite good. You should get an agent and maybe a lawyer." And I was like, "Really?" But I had little to lose.

I looked for an agent. It was grueling, going from place to place, with no idea who was telling the truth and who was lying. But in the end, Robbie Lance became my agent in New York. Inside a week's time—before flying back to Holland—I had a lawyer, an agent, and a press agent. And the cute thing about it was a month or so later I got an offer for a leading part, to be shot in Florida somewhere. It was about a man who had invented a way to attract lightning so he could use it to benefit mankind.

We accepted the offer, but two weeks later they called my new agent saying "Excuse me, sorry. The film fell apart. It's not going to happen." My agent and my lawyer said to them, "That's fine. And we are sorry. But how about the money you promised?" So they negotiated that I would get half of what the offer had been.

I was out of New York for a month and already I had a check in the mail. Fifty thousand dollars was more money than I had ever seen, and I got it for doing nothing. I was back at the farm in Holland, out of work, and I had just made more money than I had during the last five years put together.

"I think I'm going to like America," I said to my wife.

# CHAPTER 9

## UP ALL NIGHT

The bloom came off the American rose sooner than I hoped.

Making my first movie in the United States was a hard and bitter experience. Before it was over, two people close to me would be dead, and I would reach a point near despair.

It all happened suddenly—I got invitations to do two American movies, and I had to choose between them. I had taken a year off to be with my friend Marius—Ineke's brother—who was dying from Hodgkin's disease. But when I decided to try to work again, these two offers came at the same time.

The first was for something called *The Sphinx*. It was a big-budget, Hollywood-type movie. It had a seasoned and well-accepted director in Franklin Schaffner. It was a standard adventure story about a hunt for diamonds in Egypt, tied in with the mystery of the Sphinx. There were good guys, and bad guys, and betrayals and romance. There was also a French-guy role, which I was supposed to play. It was small and not that interesting. I read the script and I thought the part was a bit old-fashioned—a one-dimensional take on your stereotypical Frenchman. I didn't see where it would do anything for the film or for me.

I said, "What else have you got?"

"Well," my agent said, "Sylvester Stallone has a movie and they also want you. Stallone plays a hero New York City cop and you play a German terrorist. But we think you should do this *Sphinx* movie. It brings twice as much money, and it's going to be a bigger picture." And I said, "I think the Stallone movie is more interesting." That movie was called *Nighthawks*.

In the film I play Reinhardt Wulfgar. Wulfgar is one of the most dangerous terrorists in Europe—he has just blown up a London department store—and he chooses New York City as his next target. He undergoes plastic surgery and therefore nobody knows how he looks. A British detective, Hartman, expert in terrorism, reaches New York in order to set up a special squad to stop Wulfgar. Deke DaSilva, played by Stallone, and his partner, Matthew Fox, played by Billy Dee Williams, are two undercover cops who work the night shift and are assigned to the Wulfgar case.

A cat-and-mouse game begins, and Wulfgar succeeds in hijacking the Roosevelt Island tram, taking hostage some United Nations members and their families. In the final confrontation, Wulfgar makes his way to the apartment of DaSilva's ex-wife. She is in the kitchen, washing dishes. He sneaks in with a knife, prepared to gut her. The woman turns around, and it is DaSilva, wearing a woman's housecoat and a blond wig, and holding a big gun. As Wulfgar lunges, DaSilva shoots him, blowing him backward and out the door, where his lifeless body lands in the street.

Before I left Holland to start shooting *Nighthawks,* I said good-bye to Marius, knowing that I might not see him again. It was a decision he and I made together. I hadn't worked in nearly a year because he needed us—both Ineke and me—at home. Finally he said, "You should take on work now because this is not going anywhere and you're killing your career by just being here." I knew he was right and so I agreed.

We shot the movie in late 1979 and early 1980. It was my first serious entry into the American movie industry. We shot on location in New York City, and I was scheduled to be there for about two months. When I arrived, I saw the crew, and there were at least two hundred people working on the movie. With the size of the production, and with New York City itself—the streets and the thousands of people everywhere you looked—it was all a little overwhelming. Also, there was the fact of Sylvester Stallone himself. He was the biggest star I had ever worked with. He was a whole different order of magnitude from my European colleagues. *Rocky* had come out a few years before, and Stallone had exploded into worldwide megastardom.

Events turned sour almost from the start. Gary Nelson, who had done *The Black Hole* and a couple of other movies, was originally hired to be the director. He was a good ol' boy from Texas, and fun to be around. But the first thing I realized was that no matter who was directing, this was Stallone's movie.

Between *Rocky* and *Nighthawks,* Stallone had made a couple other films that didn't do very well. So I think he felt it was important for this one to be good. And he made everybody around him know it. He had very definite ideas, opinions, and what have you—not just about his own character, but also about everybody else's character, the story, and everything. On my first day, I learned the hard way that Stallone was, quite literally, pulling the strings.

The first scene I did was the very last scene in the movie— where I get shot and killed. I had no clue how I was going to get the character on the screen, and I had some jitters about it. I had no feel for the character yet other than just a few thoughts. What I thought I'd do was recite a poem right before I died.

I figured, "Hey, Wulfgar is a nutty guy. After he gets shot, he can speak a little of this nineteenth-century German poem." It was the Lorelei poem by Heinrich Heine, about the young maid with a broken heart who throws herself into the Rhine and becomes this sort of river mermaid who lures sailors to their deaths on the rocks. The poem begins with a line which in English means, "I don't know what to make of it." It was a ridiculous idea, all the weirder because I actually ended up doing it, and they kept some of it in the film.

It was snowing that night, and they were talking about how they wanted a really big scene for this finale. They wanted blood, and they wanted the bullets hitting me to make a real impact on the audience—I was supposed to struggle, fall all over the place, and fly through the air.

To get the effect they were looking for, they had rigged up this ninety-foot-long steel cable that went through the whole apartment from the entrance all the way through to the back exit, which was on the other side of the camera. They put me in a harness and hooked me onto the wire.

We rehearsed it a couple of times. The moment the shot went off and the bullet hit, the steel wire jerked me back suddenly. Then I had a second to catch myself, just before the next shot went off. After a couple of times, I knew what I was doing and what to expect. Everybody was pleased. Then we tried it with cameras rolling.

The first impact wrenched me sideways and knocked me through the air. There was no time to react. The next impact came before I had recovered, and then the next, both much harder than before. I was thrown around like a doll. I was startled, almost in shock.

"Cut!" somebody shouted. "Cut!"

My blood pounded. I walked over to the special effects coordinator. He was watching from the street side, just outside the front doorway. Snow was falling on his head.

"Did you change anything from the rehearsal?" I said.

His eyes went wide. He shook his head.

"Okay, who did it?"

With his head and his eyes, he sort of gestured back inside the apartment.

"Would it be Stallone?" I said.

He made a movement with his head that I took to indicate yes.

I went back inside, to the other end of the wire, where the stunt coordinator and the rest of the crew were getting ready for the next shot, and Stallone was there.

"If you ever do that again," I said, "I'm going to break your fucking balls."

It went quiet in the room. The tone was set between Stallone and me.

Later that night, in my hotel room, I felt the first stirrings of dread. This was not going to be like any shoot I had done before. I thought, "Thank God there's a director between us, who can understand me and what I'm trying to do." I felt that I had a pretty good idea what I was doing as an actor, that I would ultimately be able to give Wulfgar some depth, and that Gary believed in me and was open to my ideas.

About four or five nights later, we had to shoot this scene down in the New York subway system. Stallone and Billy Dee Williams were supposed to chase me, at high speed, through the tunnels. It was an amazing scene to shoot—the space underneath New York is vast. We were running through these endless tunnels.

That night I met Billy Dee Williams for the first time. I didn't have very much screen time with him. Billy was in the good-guy camp, so he and I didn't see each other often. It turned out he was a sweetheart—a mellow and laid-back guy. We had this sort of conversation going without saying anything—it was all in the eyes. I got the sense that he was frustrated with the situation. He was trying to do something with his character—put some depth into it—and Stallone was keeping a lid on him. From the start, there weren't many happy campers on that film.

I had heard that Stallone was a fitness fanatic, and that he trained by running up the staircases of office buildings. I had been in town for a couple of weeks and the only exercise I had managed to get was to ride my bicycle around in the snow. I didn't feel too confident as we got ready to do the scene.

I felt better very quickly. We rehearsed it, and I was running easily. It wasn't a big deal. Then Gary, with a wicked smile on take two or three, said to me, "Can you speed it up a bit?"

"You bet I can."

I guess he wanted more realism. "Well," he said, "why don't you?"

So I put a little more power in the run, and of course Stallone and Billy had to keep up. They had a hell of a time with it. I was so far ahead that we had to redo the take. So we set it up again, and I outran them just slightly. Stallone was annoyed and sulking, and inside I was smiling. The Italian Stallion and I were in this funny aggressive place together, and now Gary Nelson was my partner in crime.

For Gary it didn't work out that well.

I had the next couple of nights off, but I went to the set one night anyway. They were still in the subway, and there was a lot of tension among the crew. I could just read that Stallone was unhappy with how things were going—while Gary wasn't getting what he wanted from him. The next day, I heard that Gary had been fired. This was a week or ten days into the shoot, and my buffer was gone. But that wasn't the worst of it—not even close. Around this time, my mother died.

She was healthy and her death was unexpected. I had seen her about a month before I left Holland. We didn't see each other very often, and somehow I felt—during and after that visit—that I might not see her again. It wasn't a hair-raising type of thing—just a quiet feeling or knowing. When the call came, they altered the schedule of the film so that I could go to Holland and bury her. It was a few days before Christmas. She was seventy-one and died peacefully in her sleep, as my father would at seventy-two, two years later.

After my mother's funeral, I left again for New York. Three weeks later Marius died. Talk about a strange and terrible period. Both my mother and my best friend had died while I was away doing a movie, and I couldn't be where I wanted and needed to be. I came back from New York and I was just in time for his funeral. A few days later, I reported back on the set in New York, and my wife was with me.

The new director was Bruce Malmuth—he had made only one movie before *Nighthawks*. He was a good man, but now the show was all Stallone's. There was a representative from the Directors Guild on the set who was busy pretending not to be there—keeping his hand in front of his eyes. There are very specific union rules about who does what on a movie set— what an actor does, what the director does, what a cameraman or grip does—and one particular rule is that there can only be one director at a time. It's simple stuff, but it's clear, and in this case it was all bent out of shape. There was at least one day—maybe Malmuth hadn't gotten there yet—when Stallone himself was sitting in as the director. Even after Malmuth arrived, Stallone had his fingers in everything.

I think one of the memorable scenes for people is the one where I hijack the Roosevelt Island tram car with the United Nations people aboard. The tram is this big cable car that people use every day to commute from Roosevelt Island in the East River to Manhattan. We had the tram car every night from 2 A.M. until about 6 A.M. The delays were never-ending.

Loading the thing up would take forever, because everything had to be checked and double-checked. And everybody knew that once we were off, we were off. We didn't want to come back. We must have had twenty extras playing hostages, plus film crew. We could spend half the night just getting ready to leave.

"If you have to pee, do it now." That was our motto.

Once we finally had all the people in the car, and we got up over the river, it took more time to get everything ready. They had to get the camera in place, and get the boat in place below us when it needed to be there. So we would all wait up there, standing around in the biting cold. The car was so crowded that there wasn't any place to sit down. In the end, we were supposed to have the tram for a week, but we were so far behind that we had to go back for at least another unplanned week.

After a while, the shooting schedule started to get to me. I had just lost two people very close to me, so my mental state was not good. At some point, I decided I wasn't going to have people fuck me around too much. If I was going to do this just once in America, make just one film, I wanted to do it right. I would fight for the things I wanted. And what I wanted was to interpret my role and own my own performance, rather than have somebody telling me what to do. They had me set up as the cartoon bad guy—evil, with no explanation necessary. It was all a little too black-and-white for me. Basically, my take on it was that bad guys don't have horns on their heads. They don't have tails and a pitchfork. They can be charming. They can be sharp and businesslike. It's just that when they work, they work differently from most people.

I wasn't making this up. My character was supposed to be based on a real person—Carlos the Jackal—and I researched him when I was working with the script and getting ready for my role. This was actually an intelligent man. He was worldly, he was sophisticated, and he was elusive. He was also ruthless. He had escaped capture for years and years, often by killing the only people who knew his real identity. If you knew him, you were in trouble. He was known for walking into rooms where people immediately picked up on him, and in twenty seconds, the room fell silent. The party was over.

With all that in mind, I just thought it would be nice if my character could be at least as bright as the cop who wanted to be his enemy. Maybe he could have a conversation with the cop about *something* that somehow made sense. You know, a conversation between a cop and a terrorist in a cable tram car above the East River, and it goes something like this: "You work your side, I work my side, but what do you think the difference is? We do the same kind of job. We kill people when we have to."

That's the kind of discussion I was pushing for, and the bosses were like:

"What?"

I got my ideas from real life, but they got pretty scared for me there. They thought I was crazy. It was simple to them—terrorists were monsters. You couldn't think about what drove them. In Europe, we had already seen a lot of terrorism, so we already knew about it, and had done some thinking about it. Your enemy has motives. Your enemy has a God, too. But in America the idea was still utterly strange. Terrorism itself had rarely been dealt with—this was one of the first movies that did so. So trying to climb that mountain was tricky, and very little of it made its way into the final product. Instead, what you get is a character who kills a woman hostage on the tram, and when DaSilva asks him why he did it, he says, "I wanted to."

In the end, I went home. It was a tough job, but I got it done and I thought I did okay. I still didn't think I was going to have a career in the United States. We were living in Holland and maybe they were going to call me for another role, and maybe not. I went back to the farm. My life calmed down, I was with my loved ones, and I was glad. Life is always hectic on a movie shoot. Normal life is very different from that, and I've always relished the quiet times between shoots.

As things go, I probably needed to make *Nighthawks*. When you're from another country, there's often no other way to get started in America. Almost nobody starts out in a leading role. This is the entry door—you play a wacko, or some strange foreigner—and the victory, if you can call it that, was mine. Despite its limitations, it turned out to be a good film, and one that has not been forgotten. It did quite well among the reviewers and on cable television. People in the industry gave me a lot of credit for the work I did. Of course, just because you've had a nice role as a terrorist, it doesn't mean you're suddenly the hottest thing in town—but it does mean you can get more work.

And it wasn't long before I landed the greatest role of my career.

# CHAPTER 10

## MEETING RIDLEY

The role of my life could just as easily not have happened.

It was 1981. I had just shot a TV miniseries in Munich called *Inside the Third Reich,* in which I had the starring role as Albert Speer, one of the architects of the Nazi Final Solution. After that, I had done a film called *Chanel Solitaire* in Paris. Now I was in New York City to meet with the producers of *Das Boot.* It was the inside story of a German U-boat during World War II—a look at the war from the other side. It was eventually shot in Berlin, and it was critically acclaimed.

I had a meeting where these producers were trying to figure out if I was capable of doing their film. They had decided they liked me and wanted me. They said, "Would you be interested in the part?" I had read the script and said no.

This would be the fourth movie in a row where I played a

foreigner—and three of those roles were Germans. I wanted to escape from that. I wanted to play other roles, and I was investing my money taking English lessons so I could make it happen. Rather than learn to speak English like an Englishman, I decided to speak like an American. My thinking went like this: "There are many great British actors, the British film industry is small, and there are a limited number of roles in the United States for British actors. I can't compete there. But maybe in America I might find a place—speaking like an American."

After that failed first movie in Florida—it never even had a name—I went to Los Angeles and hooked up with the great dialogue coach Dr. Robert Easton. I worked with him for several sessions that first time. And after that, for many years, every time I got a part, I would work with him a little more. He would have me read in English and he would find the places, literally, in my mouth and in my head where I needed to rethink how I spoke.

I would do exercises with him and he would give me assignments for when I was alone and at home. He would give me tapes and have me repeat what was being said, the way it was being said. An example of an exercise might be a simple thing like saying, "Take this, that, or the other." For a Dutchman, that's really hard to say. We tend to say, "Take dis, dat, o de udda." We don't have the *th* sound in our language, or the *r* sound.

Working with languages is one of my great loves, and I was making good progress. But here I was again, talking with the *Das Boot* people about another role as a German. Had I said yes to *Das Boot*, I would have been committed to a long shoot—they did a long version of the film, and a TV series, and

in the end, it took fourteen months to make. I wouldn't have
been available for anything else. There's a factor of luck that I
see show up over and over. Or call it timing.

A couple of months passed, and I got another call. A director named Ridley Scott wanted to meet me. I happened to be
in Los Angeles. I was still living in Holland and had to pay for
hotels if I came over, which I didn't do much because I thought
it was better to just go there when they gave me a job. I didn't
go on fishing trips to Hollywood for work. I usually waited
until they called me. So there was never this casual attitude of
"Okay, now I'm here in L.A."

But I was there and Ridley wanted to meet me. I assumed
he had seen *Soldier of Orange* and *Turkish Delight* and maybe
*Nighthawks*, and was casting a film he was going to do. He
never tested me for the role—didn't feel the need. Somebody
on the inside, one of his people, had just shown him these
films of mine, and he knew he wanted me.

Ridley and I met in a little Italian restaurant he liked at the
top of Mulholland Drive somewhere. We had a light lunch and
a little coffee. We talked for three or four hours. Ridley had
sent me a script for something called *Blade Runner*. It was the
story of Deckard, a Los Angeles cop in the year 2019. He is
a "Blade Runner," a sort of assassin whose job is to kill run-
away *replicants*—genetically engineered robots that appear to be
human. The newest version—the Nexus 6—are much stronger
and more intelligent than humans. These replicants have only a
four-year life span and are used as slave labor on other planets.
They aren't allowed to return to Earth. When a group of them,
led by Roy Batty, escapes and comes back to find their inventor
and demand more time, Deckard is sent into action.

The way I remember this meeting with Ridley is that we hardly talked about the script at all. In fact, we talked about everything but *Blade Runner*. Ridley Scott is a very knowledgeable British gentleman with a good sense of humor. So he makes a pleasant eating partner, and we got along very well based on that alone. We both have a little Dennis the Menace in us, so we had common ground from the start.

I had seen two movies he had made by then—*The Duellists*, his first film, which was very good, and *Alien*, a very well-made horror film. I loved the setting, I loved the special effects, and I just thought it was a wonderful movie. After lunch, I said, "Ridley, what about this script and what about this future world and this robot stuff? I mean, can you explain what it is you see because it sounds pretty scary to me."

There were two worries that I basically had. The first one, which was the lesser one, was what the setting would look like, because everything had to be designed and created new. I find that one of the most difficult things to do is to create a totally new world from scratch that seems to have its own quality and atmosphere. Almost always, you can tell that sets are sets—that they were built for the movie. Of course, what Ridley had done with *Alien* dampened that fear somewhat.

The second, deeper concern was that there were only so many robots in movies that I had ever found convincing. I was worried that the robots would be walking funny with all this makeup on—sort of stiff and pasty-faced and ridiculous. And Ridley said, "No, no. These robots aren't like robots at all. They're like human beings, only they have to be better than human beings. I can show you some artwork."

He brought out some artwork they had done and showed

me set designs, costume designs, and a cartoonist named Enki Bilal, and we talked a little bit about Moebius, a well-known French cartoonist. I was familiar with his work. He had this style that was gritty and dark and absurd and crazy and over-the-top. At the same time, he could do stuff that was very colorful and very exotic. That's what Ridley wanted to go for—a mixture of the grim and the beautiful.

After I looked at the pictures Ridley showed me, I really got it. It clicked. I walked away from the meeting thinking things would be okay. I didn't have the part yet, but I was not afraid that I wouldn't get it. I felt that it was going to work. So I left and waited it out, and then, two weeks later, we got the call. I was hired to work on *Blade Runner*.

We were going to have two months of preproduction, and then four months of shooting. Ineke came over, and we had a nice time—living in Los Angeles. We had never gotten the opportunity because I'd never worked in L.A. I'd made a few American movies, but they had been shot in New York, Paris, and Germany. So we rented a nice large apartment in the Hollywood Hills and settled in for six months.

The original idea was that the production would have a car service pick me up in the morning and bring me home at night. But I love to drive, and will choose to drive myself whenever I can. So I said to the production people, "Can't I just have my own car? By the time you pay for this car service, I'm sure my own rental will cost less."

They agreed. Nancy Selzer—who I met after *Soldier of Orange*—worked with me for a long time. I mentioned my vehicular dilemma to her. "You know," she said. "I represent Maximilian Schell. He's got a really nice car. It's a Cadillac convertible. He's not in town right now and I'm sure he'd rent it out to you. Probably give you a good price."

It turned out to be a classic—a whale of a car, fiery red with the big fins and everything. Maximilian rented it to me for the whole six months. Not only did I get to drive that thing in to work every morning, during the little bit of time off I had, Ineke and I took it to the beach, to the mountains, and all over the place, just exploring everything Los Angeles had to offer.

With the car out of the way, I got down to work. During the two months of preproduction, I did two or three hours a day of exercise to get in shape for the role. It was important that I work out hard because I wouldn't have much time for it once shooting began. Most of the work I did was stretching, cardio, and a little bit of weight training in the gym. I did the Jane Fonda workouts in another gym. The workouts included a lot of stretching, and got your body warm, limber, and in shape.

Also during preproduction, we needed to figure out what to do with my hair. We toyed around with some ideas about the look. I'd never bleached my hair before. They'd put peroxide in my hair, then after about fifteen minutes, they'd wash it out again. The stuff burns your scalp. It feels like there's ice on there at the same time. Fire and ice—it's like a powerful hand in a steel glove is gripping your head for several hours. You have this afterglow going all day.

The peroxide leached the color from my hair and made it turn white. I began to wonder what the stuff was doing to my brain, but there was no turning back now. For the entire shoot, I had to rebleach every two or three weeks.

At the same time as all that bleaching, I worked on my

character and the script with the writer David Peoples and Ridley. It was a pleasure for me to deconstruct this character and look at his insides.

First of all, about replicants in general—I felt that they are not necessarily violent. They don't hurt anybody else unless there is no other way, just like police and soldiers do. In my mind, they are like soldiers, and spies—they are back on Earth on a mission to track down their creator and get him to give them more time. They are hiding out, avoiding confrontation. They're not a violent gang and they don't kill people unless they have to, and whether that happens is always up to the enemy. Normal people they wouldn't touch, because normal people aren't a threat. I thought that was nice—they weren't bad guys.

I also felt the Roy Batty character was written as a hero. That is what is so ironic about the movie. The protagonist, Deckard, was written as a schmuck. He is emotionally cold, a loner, maybe he's an alcoholic. And then the antagonist—Roy Batty—is written like a true warrior hero who has heart and soul and light. I mean, he's got twenty-nine qualities that you can't even find a trace of in his human opponent. The Nexus 6 special factor—this guy has all these things inside him that really don't make any sense for a machine to have—human ideals, compassion, a sense of humor, a sense of poetry and beauty. He has a conscience, it seems. He can be very affectionate—it seems that he has a heart. These are things that are great in people and even better in machines. So an illusion is created of a man, a very strong and endearing man, who is caught in a computer chip, and is running on an almost-empty battery.

This theme of having human characteristics and not being human runs all the way through the character. When he recites poetry, he doesn't understand it—it's simply a program running. He has a childlike quality to him—he is only four years old, after all. But then, in an instant, he could flex back into the captain of the ship or the assassin or whatever he needs. That's the scary part in Roy's character. He is faster than anybody—he can switch from child to soldier without needing any time. Because he is a superfast computer, and because he is just switching programs, he can change and adapt and react to things almost before they happen. Ridley made that part of the character. He said, "He does not think about reacting. He reacts instantly."

It was good that we did much of this character work beforehand. I would need to have these ideas in place because very soon, on my first day of shooting, I would have to dive right in.

# CHAPTER 11

## "FIERY THE ANGELS FELL"

I arrived at Burbank Studios early one day in March of 1981. It took me just over fifteen minutes to drive there from my apartment in the hills. It was my first day of shooting on the vast set that they had named "Ridleyville."

Walking onto the set was like being transported in time. The location was an old version of a big city that they had once used to make detective films like *The Maltese Falcon* and *The Big Sleep*. They called it the Old New York Street. Ridley and the art direction had taken the set into a serious makeover with neon lights, advertisements, elaborate overhead sprinkler machines, and all the accoutrements that would make it look like dark, futuristic, rainy Los Angeles in the year 2019.

The first scene I shot was one that comes near the end of the movie. In the scene, my character Roy Batty comes face-to-face with his maker. Eldon Tyrell, the inventor of the replicants, is the head of the massive and powerful Tyrell Corporation. Replicants only have four-year life spans, and Batty is running out of time. He has come to Earth to confront his maker and demand that he give Batty more life. This was a major scene, it would set up the important fight scene between Harrison Ford and me that would come later, and we were tackling all this at the very beginning.

Joe Turkel was the actor who played Tyrell. My first day was also his first day of shooting. Joe is a fine actor, but he couldn't seem to remember his lines. He did have some complicated lines.

So they tried it another way—they brought in some huge cue cards that he could read from. They had to make the cue cards gigantic because Joe had to wear these crazy glasses that distorted his eyes. He could barely see out of them. Even then, he had trouble reading the cards. It was years later, in fact, that I found out Joe's father was dying while we filmed the movie, but he kept it to himself.

I was quite nervous myself. Although I had done a lot of thinking about Roy Batty, I hadn't put him through his paces yet. This scene was far along in the script, and by this time in the movie, Roy's character would have been well developed. I had to play Roy in a way that was consistent with everything that had come before—the only problem being that nothing had come before.

Batty and his maker have a complex relationship. At the end of the scene, Batty kills Tyrell, and I decided I wanted to throw a curve in there before he does it. I wanted Batty to kiss him good-bye—not a peck on the cheek, but a real kiss. I mentioned it to Ridley, and he liked it. He said we'd give it a whirl. It lends the scene a strange sort of sexuality that's ironic because there's no point in having that in a robot. What struck me when I got to Los Angeles was that everybody there was so much into their sexuality, whatever that was—you have all kinds of varieties—and I thought, "What is all that about?" So I decided to play with that.

For Batty, his sexuality is all the way around and even that doesn't matter because he's a machine—he literally doesn't have any use for it. It's just part of the makeup and he kisses his sister as he kisses his father as he kisses his brother, and if it's on the tongue or on the cheek, it doesn't matter—it's just the way of the program that says "love."

Shortly before filming, we heard that they were going to cut a few scenes later in the script. The way the script was originally written, Roy would kill Tyrell by squeezing his head and jamming his fingers in Tyrell's eyes. Tyrell would fall to the ground and his head would split open, with wires and smoke coming out—revealing that Tyrell was actually a replicant himself. After this, Roy would discover the real Tyrell—long dead and frozen in a block of ice. The company had created a replicant Tyrell to serve as its public face and keep stock prices high.

It was decided to cut the part about the block of ice so that the first Tyrell that Batty encounters becomes the real Tyrell. The difference being that Roy kills his maker instead of killing a Tyrell look-alike to get to the real maker—a big difference. Also, we still had the head to contend with. They had made this fake Tyrell head and they wanted to use it. Even though the scene had been changed, I was still supposed to crush the toy head, stick my fingers in its eyes, and have the blood run out of it. They thought it would look more real to do it that way, but the gadget head was high-tech and complicated, and it had one other obvious downside—it wasn't attached to Joe Turkel's body.

"Ridley," I said, after playing with the toy on camera a few times, "can't I just squeeze Joe's head?"

Once we did that, it became much easier to shoot. I had these bloody sponges glued to my fingers and thumbs, and I just slipped them in behind his glasses where the camera couldn't see them. I sort of put them over his eyes, but never really squeezed that much.

I was already feeling more confident. It was a tough first day, but the director had liked my characterization and my ideas. I got a warm feeling from Ridley, and I knew we had done some good work.

All movies have delays, and *Blade Runner* is legendary for it. As time passes, you start to get a sense of the delays and what they'll be like. It gets so that you could gamble on them. Eight times out of ten you'd be right. They come to your trailer and say, "It'll be another half hour." So you look at your watch and say, "Okay, that means they'll come back in an hour and a half." In an hour and a half, they come back and say, "It's going to be ten more minutes." That means they'll be back in half an hour. In half an hour, they come and say, "Two minutes. We need you in two minutes." Now it's getting close.

With *Blade Runner*, because the lighting would take so much time, the delays were long. I'd sit for a couple of hours, then go shoot for an hour. Then I'd sit for another couple of hours, then go shoot again. To put the downtime to good use,

I was reading the script in my trailer, thinking about the part, adding some playfulness and getting a grip on it.

I do remember one day when I didn't have a scene, but came in to watch them film. Throughout my career, I've done this from time to time because of my desire to do some directing—when I'm on a film with a great director, it's like my homework to study his or her moves. When I came in that day, they were doing the scene where Deckard first gives Rachael the test to see if she's a replicant. It takes place in this gigantic room with a view of Los Angeles, and he turns the lighting down to register her irises better. Ridley was after this effect that the curtains in the room were almost like digital curtains. Whatever he was getting from them wasn't what he wanted, and it took forever to finally get it right. In fact, they spent hours on it, and then I watched them shoot just one little segment.

People have described friction on the set between the actors, the crew, the directors, everybody. I felt that there was some tension now and then, but that's normal. Tension doesn't mean it's not going well. People get tired on long shoots. It happens on every movie and it didn't faze me. The fact is I was on my own most of the time. Which isn't to say that I cloistered myself. For the most part, I just had good relationships with the people that I met.

Brion James, who played the replicant Leon, was a friend of mine. He was one of the first people I met in Los Angeles. I had met him by chance in Marina Del Rey, and we would go out from time to time, for a coffee or a beer, and shoot the shit about the movies and motorcycles, or whatever else came to mind. When he showed up for the part, I thought, "Oh, that's fun." We had a real strong rapport and it was good to be a team. We worked together on *Flesh + Blood* and a couple of other projects after *Blade Runner*. And for years, I would see him when I was in town. He is a great man.

We had a funny scene together where Batty and Leon go to see the man who makes the eyes for the replicant. The guy's name is Chew, played by the veteran actor James Hong. Chew has this little lab he works out of, and it has to be cold in there to protect all these eyes he's making. We shot that scene inside a meat locker in an industrial part of L.A. The temperature inside the meat locker was turned way down. They wanted to see our breath. Chew got to wear winter clothes inside there, but since Leon and I were robots, we had to wear our street clothes and act like the cold didn't affect us. We both had long underwear on, but the cameras were starting to freeze. Of course, when we stepped outside for a break, it was an eighty-five-degree day in downtown Los Angeles. Meanwhile, Brion is doing all these antics that made it into the movie, like sticking his hand in some goo, sniffing it, and not liking the smell. It was just Brion goofing around.

There was some nice poetry in that scene. "Fiery the angels fell. Deep thunder rolled around their shores, burning with the fires of Orc." I have no idea what Blake meant by that, but it seemed to make perfect sense.

I remember that I was acting out my stuff in the icebox scene and Ridley said, "Rutger, do it slower. Take a ton of time with each line." I'd never done anything like that before—in fact, Paul Verhoeven used to tell me to speed it up. So now I was drawing out every word, speaking like, "Where . . . would . . . I . . . find . . . this . . . man?" I thought he would never use that take in the movie, but that's the one he used, and it works.

Then I had my few scenes with Daryl Hannah. She plays a replicant, a pleasure model named Pris. Roy and Pris are lovers, but again, it's more complicated than that. I told her, "I'm the soldier and I'll protect you. But we're also pals. We're like sisters—sisters, lovers, it doesn't matter, because we're robots."

Daryl was like my little sister. She was about nineteen years old at the time—like a kid, and very girlie. This was before she did *Splash* and *Steel Magnolias* and became a worldwide star. She had been a model before *Blade Runner*, and had done a couple of movies. We were another team together because she started mimicking me. She studied me and began taking over a little bit of my walk and the way I smoked and the way I looked. She was startling sometimes.

I would visit the set to see the others work sometimes. I remember she was doing a scene with Sebastian, played by William Sanderson, who became famous for his funny portrayal of a country bumpkin on the *Newhart* show. Few people can forget his signature line on that show—"I'm Clarence, this is my brother Darrell, and this is my other brother Darrell." Sebastian was a recluse because he had a disease that made him age too quickly—he was ashamed of the way he looked. Whatever else he was, Sebastian was a genius inventor for the Tyrell Corporation, and he was Roy's key to getting into the heavily fortified Tyrell Building. Pris is the decoy that gets Sebastian to let down his guard.

Their first scene together is one of the most beautiful in the movie. It's the one where Sebastian comes upon Pris, who is hiding in the alley outside his home. She runs away, but crashes into Sebastian's car. Daryl really did run into the car, and hit it so hard that her hand went through the window. That made the scene very real.

There was one actor who I didn't have scenes with, but with whom I made a pretty good connection. That was Edward James Olmos, in his pre–*Miami Vice* days. He played Gaff, another Blade Runner, who sort of shadows the lead Blade Runner around in the story. I would see him on the set from time to time, and we'd have a little chat.

Early on, he said, "Oh, man. I love your eyes. I'd love to have eyes like that. I wanted to play this role with blue eyes." He has dark brown eyes and I felt by saying that, he was just being genuine with me.

"That's no problem," I said. "Get contact lenses."

"I know. They have different ones now. You can have any color you want. But the production won't pay for them. They say I don't need them."

"Why don't you just pay for them yourself?"

"Well," he said. "I don't think they'll let me."

"Just try, and see what happens."

My saying that might have helped him a little bit. I think Olmos must have pushed them because a short time later he turned up wearing one blue contact lens. He did an amazing job with his character—making it stand out despite not having that much screen time—and that one blue eye just takes the sweetest part of the cake.

All the replicants had contacts. We had these specially made contacts that would go over the entire eyeball—there was a certain effect Ridley wanted. Now and then, he wanted the light to hit a replicant's eyes a certain way, and reflect back a red glint. It would give away the fact that this person was a replicant.

So we would do a scene—and then do the scene over again with the contacts in. First, they had to numb your eye with some painkiller drops. Then they'd put these huge contacts on you—they were like blast shields. You could hardly see anything—like really dark sunglasses.

Ridley's painstaking approach led a few people to feel like pulling their hair out dealing with him, but I never felt that way. In fact, I felt great making *Blade Runner*. Ridley really did let us play with the characters, and I felt that I had a special place with him. When that connection happens it becomes easy to work and everything just flows. This was one of my first movies in America, and it was a serious role. I came in there doubting myself, but I had no doubts about what Ridley was doing. He inspired confidence and he gave me the freedom to be creative.

I kept thinking about Roy and getting ideas that I would bring to work. Ridley would say, "Yes, let's try it," or "No, let's not do that." Ridley wanted a robot that was more human than humans, so I asked, "Can I put things in him like a sense of smell, like a sense of beauty, like a feeling for poetry that he doesn't understand but somehow it's there, all the elements I can come up with?" And Ridley said, "I like it—keep going." So it became like picking through a salad bowl, looking for things to include.

After a while, you could feel it while we were shooting—

as all the characters started to play their roles, the replicants started to become more fun, more alive, and more human than the human beings in the movie. That becomes most clear in the final scenes, when Roy finally meets Deckard, that most dreary and despicable human of all.

# CHAPTER 12

## TEARS IN RAIN

I barely even saw Harrison Ford.

We worked for four months on the same movie, we were the two main enemies, but we worked together just a few days a month.

Our action sequence took about three weeks to shoot. In that sequence, Pris dies, and Batty has a confrontation with Deckard, played by Harrison. Their battle finishes with a chase in the pouring rain through decaying buildings, and across rooftops and ledges high above the city. Batty is the superior warrior, but his batteries are running down, his four-year lease on life is up, and he has compassion for the weaker Deckard and lets him live. Batty dies peacefully on a rooftop with the beaten and battered Deckard lying nearby, watching.

During these final scenes, Roy could kill Deckard at any

time, but he's just messing with him, one warrior testing the other warrior to see if he will come up to his level. Deckard, who earlier in the film shot a woman in the back, never steps up. Roy dies trying to kick some spirit into this pathetic cop.

In the original script, instead of a chase sequence, there was a fight in a gymnasium, Bruce Lee style, between Batty and Deckard. I'm not Bruce Lee, and I didn't feel I could make that work. I could practice for years and I still wouldn't be Bruce Lee. I also felt that we had already seen about twenty-nine fights like that in twenty-nine different movies, so why do it again?

"Why don't you make it a chase?" I said to Ridley. "Almost like a dance of life and death?" We worked that idea through, played with it, and we liked it.

During the sequence Deckard was on the other side of the wall, or in another room, or running away—I was playing in the dark by myself much of the time. There's a scene where he hits me over the head, and there's another one where he's hanging from the roof and I save his life. There wasn't much dialogue in either scene, and our main goal was to make sure neither of us got hurt. Our interactions amounted to "Okay, you hit me like this and then I'll go like this. Yeah? Okay."

I never hear Harrison talk about *Blade Runner*—it's almost like it doesn't exist to him. Of course, when you're a professional actor, all that stuff doesn't matter that much.

At times, when a production is behind schedule, you get people from the movie studio coming over going "What's going on here?" They're hovering around, looking over the director's shoulder. Even worse, sometimes you get people from the bond company—the people who have guaranteed the money to complete the job. They're like the fire-breathing dragons coming—nobody looks forward to it. If you're over budget, they have to pay for it, and they want to make sure you don't screw around. They're like black ravens perched there, and they were on the set of *Blade Runner*.

To add to the fun, a possible Actors Guild strike was looming. If the strike came, and we weren't done, it would be a disaster—actors would have to stop working on the project and the whole thing would stall until the strike was over. So we had a deadline, and we were working long hours to beat it.

The last days were especially long. During the fight sequence, Roy sheds his clothes—he turns up in a scene and suddenly he is almost naked. I interpreted it as a show of true color and peeling away his skin. Roy getting naked made my days so long since it meant I had two extra hours of makeup each day. When Roy takes his clothes off, he has markings all over his body—mysterious tattoos on his chest, arms, and neck with all these letters and numbers, and if you look closely in the light, the tattoos seem to glow because they're actually computer chips and connection openings.

I ended up doing stunts in the final sequence—there was one in particular that I wasn't supposed to do, and it nearly got out of hand. In the scene, Roy jumps across the alley from one roof to another. The setup was nice because the first building was a little higher than the second one—you wouldn't have to jump straight across. You jumped down, and while it looked like a good distance, the buildings weren't terribly far apart— or so it seemed until the first stunt guy tried it and didn't make it. He fell and he hurt himself—not seriously, but it did put him out of commission for that scene. A second stuntman made another attempt and hurt himself as well. Meanwhile, the setup for this kind of thing takes hours, the night was burning away, and that strike was coming. A gloom settled over the crew.

"Ridley," I said, "I don't know if you're with me on this, but if they can get the building a foot closer to the other side, I can do it. I know I can."

I knew that they had constructed the buildings on big rollers, so I knew they could move them closer. I guess they were desperate enough that finally he said, "Okay."

Of course, he took a big risk—the risk that I'm full of shit. If I'm lying, or if I make a mistake and fall, we have even bigger problems than before. All I need to do is twist my ankle and the production grinds to a halt. But we did it. They rolled the buildings a little closer together, I made the leap, and it was fine. The crew gave me some applause afterward, I got some credit from the stuntmen.

There were two shots in that final sequence that I didn't want to do. Earlier in the shoot, Ridley and I had talked quite a bit about the danger of turning the replicants into gods or superheroes—we had agreed that we didn't want to do that. Of course, there's reality and then there's movie reality, and they are very different. In movies, supposedly normal people do things that people in the real world could never pull off, and that's fine. If done right, it's part of the fun—as viewers, we want our movie characters to be more than we are. All the same, we had decided it would feel contrived and over the top if these robots were capable of too much.

Then came the fight sequence with Harrison. In one scene,

Deckard is hanging from a building by one hand. At some point he can't hold on any longer, but Roy catches him by the arm and drags him up onto the roof. It's impossible in real life. To me, this wasn't so bad because we'd established that Roy is fast. If you shoot at him, he's anticipated that you're going to—so by the time you pull the trigger he's gone. Action and reaction being the same.

The more glaring problem here is the fact that Roy brings Deckard onto the roof. There's no man who can ever lift another man by one arm and pull him up like that. If someone goes over the edge, and you catch him, he's going to pull you down with him, and not the other way around. The only way you could lift him back up is if you're anchored to something, and even then only if you get him with both hands and you're almost impossibly strong. He weighs two hundred pounds, you weigh two hundred pounds—you're pulling your own weight up, against gravity, with no leverage, no time to set yourself, and with nothing but the strength in your arms. You'd have to have forearms and wrists like Popeye to even arrest his fall in the first place. Thank God Nexus 6 was really a machine and had a built-in bonus surprise factor; he was more human than humans.

The other moment I was reluctant about was the scene when Roy sticks his head through the wall. The wall itself was well prepared—very thin, balsa-type wood with foam on the inside—and I put my head right through it, three takes without a problem. But in between takes, I wondered about it.

I said, "Ridley, do we have to do it this way?"

"We cannot do it another way."

"But it's too much. It's just too much."

"Rutger, trust me," he said. "It looks wonderful."

On the day before the strike deadline, we shot for twenty-five hours straight. It was a race to finish the movie, and the tension was high. We were trying to do the final rooftop scene where Batty dies.

The film was coming to an end and we had been working at an incredible pace for weeks, under the rain machines the whole time. I had reached my breaking point. People were so tired that they were making a lot of mistakes. Lighting mistakes, prop mistakes, mistakes with the camera—problems would arise and the solution wouldn't come to anyone. We would stand there with time passing, with no answer because no one was thinking straight anymore. Meanwhile, I was soaking wet the whole time.

Twenty-five hours on the set, and we had at least another eight hours to go. I just couldn't do it anymore. "Ridley," I said, "I'm sorry but I'm going home now. I want to go to sleep."

As I walked away, I could feel this sense of "Oh my God!" happening among the people behind me, but I just kept going and didn't stop until I got home. The next day, after I had slept, I telephoned the set. We'd gotten lucky. "The strike didn't happen," they said, "and we're gonna finish the movie tonight." That's when I sat down and found the ending.

As scripted, the ending was a page-long monologue with a lot of high-tech language. I wasn't that happy with it. We'd had these operatic death scenes for all the other replicants, and I thought that was enough. I also felt Ridley and I had agreed earlier that when the batteries go, they go. There's no red light going off, there's no good-bye, there's just the dead replicant.

Everybody dies before they're ready, Roy Batty included,

so I cut thirty of his lines. I saved two because I felt there was some poetry and some mystery in there. And I added the last line, "All those moments will be lost in time, like tears in rain."

When I got in, everybody had gotten some sleep and the mood was much improved. The last night of shooting, the real last night, was a happy night—people now were professionals giving their best again, and they could see that they were doing something really beautiful with the ending of the film.

What I love about the final sequence is that Roy performs an act of kindness and compassion—saving Deckard's life. At the moment Deckard falls, Roy grabs. He doesn't really have a reason for doing it. In the last speech, which is a speech that a lot of people like, he's still just running programs. For instance, he says, "All those moments will be lost in time," and before he says "like tears in rain," I have him swallow as if he's emotionally choked up. But in my mind, I did that because it's in his program. He's saying these final swan-song lines, and now it says in his program, "You have to swallow, Roy." And he goes, "*Unc*, like tears in rain." This is a real Nexus 6 bonus moment which would have pleased his maker. Roy is never a hero, but for one moment he acts like one.

The dove that I hold in that scene came about randomly—it was just an idea that occurred to me. The chase went through a room where Deckard and Roy passed some doves. I told Ridley, "I know it's not in the script, but I want Roy to grab a dove as a toy, a last companion holding on to life and peace. And when he dies, he lets it go, and it flies away, like the soul is leaving his body." I wanted to let the dove do the rest of the acting for me.

Ridley agreed, but he wasn't sure, so we shot it two ways—one without the dove and one with it. When we shot it with the dove, things didn't go quite as planned. It was cold and rainy on that roof, and my hand was probably warm. I was sitting there, and all I needed to do was just let it go. My head dropped, Roy died, and I let go of the dove, but it didn't fly—it wasn't moving at all. It was just lying there in my hand.

I was like "Aw jeez, come on now." I shook my hand a bit, but the dove didn't budge, so I shook it again. This time, the dove got up, walked along my thigh, jumped off onto the surface of the roof, and walked off. That's why in the movie, there's an extra shot of the dove flying up. They shot that additional footage in postproduction, all because the bird didn't perform very well. I'm smiling as I write this.

At the time we shot *Blade Runner,* I had very little experience with American moviemaking. This was a big film and a big experience, but I didn't really know what to expect. I went back to Holland and waited nearly a year until the release of the film.

# CHAPTER 13

## AFTER *BLADE RUNNER*

On a warm night in June of 1982, I went to the premiere of *Blade Runner* in Los Angeles. I don't remember doing any press appearances or promotion beforehand. I think the studio execs were nervous. It had gone through a few different edits by then—and audience reactions at sneak previews had been mixed. I felt uncertain about it myself.

Then I saw it, and I was just blown away by the Vangelis score, the incredible camera and artwork, the special effects and story. I thought it was just brilliant. The sound track added an extra dimension.

I felt that we had gotten a film with more layers than we were even thinking of. I knew right away that this was a very different and special movie. I thought it was great. Life is how you look at it, and *Blade Runner* decided to look at it in a poetic but dark way and, at the same time, with a lot of wit. It was not consumer-ready crap and it was not a fast-paced, science-fiction thriller. Instead, it was thoughtful and slow moving, and it challenged audiences to enter its world.

Half the audience loved it and the other half hated it. Nobody felt lukewarm about it and that was clear. It felt as if there was a strike of lightning going through the audience. People cheered because they thought it was wonderful. People moaned because they thought it was terrible. But everybody came out stunned. I remember walking down these stairs—it was on Hollywood Boulevard—and I heard this woman's voice behind me. She said, "That's not the L.A. we know. It's so depressing." Well, what are you going to do? You can't please everybody. All I knew was that I was quite pleased.

The scene that sums up the magic of moviemaking is the one where Deckard is analyzing a photograph with a machine called an Esper. He found some photos in Leon's hotel room, and he's using the Esper to enhance the images and search through them for clues. Everything about this scene winks to the audience and says, "Watch me create a lie."

For one, there is an image of Roy Batty sitting at the table in the pose of Rodin's *Thinker*. This was funny to me because it's silly for a robot to have a sense of humor about a famous sculpture from the past—it's silly for him to even know about it. What's even funnier is that the Roy Batty in *The Thinker* pose isn't always Roy—sometimes it's a stuntman dressed like Roy. I wasn't on the set when they shot all of that.

Then Deckard uses the Esper to go deep into one of the photos. First he enlarges the reflection on a glass. Then he enlarges the reflection on a vase. Then he enlarges the reflection on an old French period mirror which itself distorts the image. This mirror is called trompe l'oeil, which means "deceive the eye" because it distorts the image it reflects. In that bent reflection, he travels farther and deeper into the picture and he finds a bed with a woman lying on it—the woman is Zhora. In the process of going deep into these reflections, he manages to turn our vision almost 360 degrees—with the loss of light in each reflection, what he's doing is just about impossible. As a viewer, your eye is really being cheated here, all the more so because the Zhora in the photo isn't Joanna Cassidy. Joanna had finished her scenes by the time they shot this, so she was already long gone. The Zhora in the photo is a stuntwoman. The whole idea was for Deckard to be able to recognize Zhora once he'd seen her.

So the truth of all of this is that the scene is full of lies. I love it because it's so close to what we do as filmmakers. We show you a story as we see it and, at the same time, it's a total illusion that's full of cracks and not a little humor. *Blade Runner* is like that in every detail.

No matter, the movie was out of the theaters within a few weeks. It was gone just like that—and it's important to remember that this was in a very different time from today. In 1982, a movie didn't have to be a hit right away—it was normal to give people a chance to tell their friends about it—but the company jerked *Blade Runner* out of the movie houses immediately.

Some influential critics hated it—Janet Maslin, Pauline Kael, Roger Ebert, and several others gave it bad reviews. It was a disappointment to see the film die that way, but then an interesting thing started to happen. It didn't happen right away—it unfolded slowly, gradually building over a period of years. In the early 1980s, two fairly new technologies were just beginning to reach into many homes—cable television and home video. Those developments started to give films a chance to be seen again after they left the theaters. People who missed *Blade Runner* in the theaters saw it first on cable. Then they began to rent it and buy it at video stores. It began to find its audience, and over time, that audience grew and became more passionate. It became one of the most rented videos of the decade.

Ten years passed with *Blade Runner* simmering on a back burner. In 1992, Warner Brothers announced that they would rerelease *Blade Runner* for a limited theater run. The version they would release was a director's-cut version—Ridley had reedited and put it together in a way that the producers wouldn't let him do the first time. This would also be his chance to make some money—he never made much money on the first release.

I went to a Los Angeles screening. The place was packed and there was real excitement in the air—people were hot for *Blade Runner*. It was a wonderful surprise to find that the audience had revived a movie that the studio had killed. Since then, the film has taken on a life of its own. People have spent hundreds of millions of dollars buying it and renting it—and buying products associated with it. It has made many critics' top-ten lists, has been included in the Library of Congress film archives, and recently *Wired* magazine called it the greatest science-fiction movie of all time.

A question I still get asked even now is what I think of the different versions. I think there are three major changes from the first to the second version, and that two of them are positive—the last one I'm not so sure about.

The first change is that in the director's-cut version, they got rid of the voice-over. In the original release, Harrison Ford as Deckard does this narrative—a 1930s Sam Spade kind of thing—that I never liked. He just goes on and on, saying, "I wonder, I wonder—I had a feeling and it really confused me and I don't know what's happening." It's like the voice-over is trying to explain things to you that you can understand without its help. Without the voice-over—and to me that's the biggest difference—the film just moves on its own, maybe a little slower but more powerful.

The second difference between the two is that in the director's cut, they eliminated the very last scene—some flyover footage that really didn't belong there. The first time around, it ended by having Deckard run away with the beautiful replicant Rachael in his fly car. He has fallen in love with Rachael—a "pleasure model"—who Tyrell was treating as his own daughter. What happened was the producer owned some aerial flyover footage that was left from the movie *The Shining*.

It's not an end that fits the movie, and in more ways than one. The whole film has a very specific look, then suddenly you get these flyover shots that are very different in photography. Also, this is a dark movie, and they tried to glue this happy Hollywood ending on at the end. "They flew away together and lived happily ever after." I don't know who made the decision, but to me it's a joke because one of the people flying away is a sophisticated sex toy—a blow-up doll, but made out of Nexus texture. For the detective to go "Well, I just lost it and fell in love," that's a Hollywood bullshit ending. Basically, it's a guy that flies off with his blow-doll, gives you the thumbs-up, and says "Hey, life's short!" Cutting that ending is a big improvement.

The third major change in the director's cut is a scene that was added. This is the change that I'm not sure about. They added a scene where Deckard has a dream of a unicorn running in a field. Later, the other detective character, Gaff, leaves an origami statue of a unicorn. A lot has been said about this, but probably the only way that Gaff can know Deckard dreams of unicorns is if Deckard is himself a replicant and Gaff knows his programming.

I never really understood this change—mostly because I didn't want to. I didn't really like it because if Deckard himself is a machine, then the whole story of a battle of wits and wills between man and machine dies for me. It is such a classic story to tell, and it is told here in a way that is compelling. To me, *Blade Runner* investigates what life and what being human are about—and the investigation is done by Roy rather than Deckard.

Whatever the version, I consider Roy Batty the greatest role of my career, and *Blade Runner* the greatest movie I've been in. People have often asked me what I might do to top it, or how will I do it again, or will it bother me if I never top it. It's an interesting question, and one that is hard to answer. To be a genius even once in life is not a given, and when it happens it usually comes together because of forces outside our control. So many different variables have to fall into place independently that you might as well say it was good luck.

How do you make the best wine? It's in the soil. It's in

the water. It's in the air and the temperature, and we used a little bit of this and that and the other and, shit, it turned out to be the best wine. A diamond comes about because of a lot of factors—so many that you can't even know what they all are. You can't make Diamond 2 and have it be the same as the original.

*Blade Runner* definitely changed my life. It is a relatively early film, at least in my English-speaking career, and I knew after seeing it that I had done a good job. As times goes on and people keep responding to it in such a positive way, it reinforces my first instinct that this is a great movie—one that is beautiful, dark, wicked, poetic, exotic, and beautiful.

It's great for an actor to learn that you've made a connection with an audience, especially a worldwide audience—that's what you hope for when you're making a movie. If the film's still alive twenty-five years later, and that connection is still there, that's genius—it's an opportunity and a privilege given to very few people.

# CHAPTER 14

## THE BEST ROLE I DIDN'T GET

One day in the late summer of 1983, I was home in Holland and I got a call from the director Richard Donner. Dick is a bighearted bear of a man, and a good director with great instincts—almost like a bloodhound, he makes wonderful movies by smelling his way to the right place. In recent years he had done some very popular films, including *The Omen* and the first two *Superman* movies. When I picked up the phone, he started talking.

"Rutger, we're here in Rome and we'd like to ask you a question."

"Hello, Dick. That sounds nice. How's it going?" I had actually never been to Italy.

"Well," he said. "Not so good."

"Oh? Sorry to hear that."

"Lauren and I are on the set of *Ladyhawke*. I'm ten days from the start of principal photography, and we're having some problems. Kurt Russell just left. Remember Navarre?"

"Sure," I said.

A year earlier, in Los Angeles, Dick had invited me for a conversation about *Ladyhawke*. I thought the script was magic. It was an adaptation of a medieval legend that had been around in one form or another since the thirteenth century.

*Ladyhawke* is the story of the knight, Etienne Navarre, and his lover, the beautiful Isabeau. The two are victims of a spell cast by the Bishop of Aquila. The Bishop had wanted Isabeau for his wife, and when she chooses Navarre instead, the Bishop decides they will never have each other. By day, Isabeau is a hawk, and rides on Navarre's arm. At night, she becomes a woman again, but Navarre takes on the form of a wolf. They are doomed to wander the countryside, always together but forever apart. When they meet Philippe, a thief who has escaped from the Bishop's dungeon, they find hope that they can free themselves from the dark curse.

After reading the script, I went in to talk with Dick and with Lauren Schuler, the producer. By then, Lauren had been trying for a couple of years to bring this story to the screen. An enchanting aside is that she first met Dick while putting *Ladyhawke* together, convinced him to be the director, and while working together on the film, they fell in love and eventually got married. *Ladyhawke* was the spark to their romance.

Dick and Lauren asked me if I wanted to play THE BAD GUY. They already had someone to play Navarre—Kurt Russell, the star of *Escape from New York* and *The Thing*. I did not want the bad-guy role. It was not interesting to me. It was stupid, almost a cliché.

I thought, "If they don't consider me as the main character, then I'm not going to do some bad-guy role that I don't like, and that I think is boring." I expressed this to them, as well as that I thought I was quite good for the Navarre role and that if they ever changed their minds, I would be delighted to come back anytime they asked.

"So what do you think?" Dick said now, over the phone. "Are you available, and do you still want to play Navarre?"

"What? Of course. I'll see you in a couple of days," I said. "Make sure they have a parking space for my fifty-five-foot tractor trailer!"

As Dick and Kurt Russell had started to work on the film, each of them just didn't feel comfortable with the other. Then Kurt sort of left the set and negotiated his way out of the contract. It may seem a strange way to get a part, but in this case, just because Kurt and Dick couldn't hack it together, I got lucky.

Dick thought I was kidding about the tractor trailer, but I wasn't. I owned a big eighteen-wheeler, which I still have to this day. I bought it in 1977. I bought a truck and a container box, and I built a house in it. I put a marble floor in there. I put a washing machine in there, and a dryer, and a kitchen, and a sitting area, and a bathroom, and a shower, and a bedroom. It became like a one-bedroom apartment inside a forty-foot container. I even put in a five-hundred-gallon freshwater tank, and a five-hundred-gallon black water tank underneath the chassis. I like building and designing stuff myself. And the whole idea of taking my living room and having the view change just charms me to death.

I've made fifteen movies with the truck, mostly in Europe, and it's been a great adventure. For *Flesh + Blood*, a medieval movie I made with Paul Verhoeven in 1985, I drove it to Spain—and it got broken into three times. The police said it was drug addicts, trying to steal whatever they could find. Usually, they just broke a window when we weren't around. One night was like something out of a nightmare. It was February and snow was on the ground.

Ineke was with me. Both of us were sleeping, but she's a light sleeper and I'm not. In the middle of the night, she heard a sound. Totally naked and very beautiful, she climbed out of bed to investigate . . . and found this guy standing in the middle of our living room. I woke up when I heard her scream.

"I'm gonna fucking kill you!" she shouted. She went after him with this little baseball bat that we had near the bed, and chased him into the night. Moments later, I was just getting out of bed, rubbing my eyes.

"What's going on?"

There was my wife, standing naked with a baseball bat in her hands. I stared at her. It all seemed so weird.

"What are you looking at?" she said.

"Aren't you cold?" I said.

After I got the call from Dick Donner, I loaded up the eighteen-wheeler and started driving. Fifteen hundred miles—I got there in three days. I put the airbrakes on right in front of the main gate of the famous Cinecittà Studios in Rome. Dick came storming out the door, his big voice booming across the street, "RUTGER, what the . . . ? GODDAMN!"

His voice lowered. "I don't know," he said, "but I don't think you can park that thing here."

I smiled. "I'll move it first thing in the morning."

Before I left home, I had hoisted a motorcycle into the small parking space I have inside the front of the truck, and I could lower the bike and just sniff out the neighborhood. On the bike I could find out the routes to take to get the truck up the hill, around the corner, and back into a really nice spot. So at six o'clock in the morning, when there was no traffic, I moved the truck to a better place. I ended up parking it on a hillside looking out over Rome—from my bed, I could look straight across at the pope's quarters.

Dick showed me the sets for the production. They were magnificent. They had built the biggest secular cathedral ever, 250 feet long, towers 80 feet high, made out of hardboard, plaster, real stone, and tiles—an awe-inspiring structure. The climactic scene of the movie would take place there, and building that set was an enormous project that had taken months. It had to be built because we couldn't shoot in a real medieval church—where there are too many frescoes, icons, and artifacts that need to be protected.

My two main costars in this movie were Matthew Broderick, who would play the thief Philippe, and Michelle Pfeiffer, who would play Isabeau. Although Philippe was supposed to be a boy in his early teens, Matt was actually a young man in his early twenties when we shot the movie—he has a gift for seeming eternally young. He had been a successful stage actor in New York City before he turned to the movies—he'd had two Broadway triumphs back-to-back in the Neil Simon plays *Brighton Beach Memoirs* and *Biloxi Blues*. When we were working on *Ladyhawke,* the film *War Games* had just come out, where he plays a teenage hacker who nearly starts World War III. It was a big hit, and Matt was riding high.

In the story, I have my lover Isabeau on my arm in the form of a bird. When she takes human form, I become a wolf, so we never see each other. Philippe takes up with me, travels with me, and through him I am able to speak with my lover, and know about her. He is the only one who can communicate with both of us. For me, he becomes a sort of substitute or surrogate for her. In a sense, he becomes part of my lover. I was curious to see what he would do with that.

I was hoping for a Shakespearean feel to his character, a sort of androgynous, Annie Lennox thing happening. But when Philippe was talking about Isabeau, there was too much male in there. At the same time, with Michelle, I felt he really was trying to be the man there, too. Since most of my scenes were with him, I was pretty lonely at times—but that was okay for my character because Navarre was lonely, too.

I barely saw Michelle. We had only a couple of scenes together. As it is on most shoots, when the long day is over people disappear to their hotel rooms and to that small part of their own life they get to keep. My experience is that you might meet your colleagues briefly before you shoot, and while you're working you just meet on the set. By then the roles are taking over. Still, I did feel close to her—much in the same way Navarre feels close to Isabeau though he never sees her. It was almost like we were the same person.

Of course, Michelle and I did have our one big scene together—at the end. I had quite a few lengthy talks with Dick Donner about the end scene, and what two lovers do when they see each other again, other than just embrace. I wanted to find something that would immediately prove that the love between them was just as it was before, and that time lost really didn't matter. I was looking for something small and subtle.

"Don't worry about it," Dick said. "You just have to embrace her and that's it. People will get the idea."

Then it came out that Michelle had been playing with the whole idea of her character having wings—Isabeau had been a bird and should somehow have wings as a result. Michelle wanted to get the wings and the whole bird thing into her performance. For instance, she had this fetish about the little ties that were around the hawk's legs to keep him on your arm. She really made a point in one of the last scenes by dropping these in front of the Bishop, basically saying, "I am released from all the ties of your curse."

Although we hadn't interacted much, I had seen her around the set. It came to me that with her beauty and with her size, she was a lot like a bird herself. She was tiny, and very slim. We'd shot the final scene already, where I embrace her, and I said to Dick, "Let's do one more take. I want to try something." And to Michelle I said, "I'll lift you really high. Let's see you fly." We did it, and I lifted her up really high. She was light as a feather and that's where she spreads her wings.

Michelle and I also had a photo shoot together on the very last day. They wanted a publicity photo with both of us on the horse. So we climbed up on the horse, and the whole thing nearly ended in disaster.

I had trained to work with this particular horse, Othello, who was nineteen years old. This horse was very sensitive in its mouth and I was too firm with the reins in my hand. He was just trying to get away from the pain, so he did what came naturally—he reared up high and he fell over backward.

Thankfully, Michelle was thrown clear, but I wasn't. For me, the saddle was almost like a prison—I had a long sword on one side, and this double-barreled crossbow on the other. I was only halfway off the horse when we hit the ground, and he landed on my leg. If we had been on solid ground, he would have smashed my leg bone. But we were on grass, so I walked away again. No damage to the horse, no damage to me. Is there anything more rewarding than good luck?

There is a scene when the wolf and the bird are both human and they almost touch. It's a miracle moment in time where the sun is just peeking over the horizon, but it's still nighttime. They are both human for a split second, then they lose each other again. We shot that scene on location in the mountains—part of the Italian Alps. We were above seven thousand feet, there was snow all around, dry mountain air, and the temperature was below zero. Way below zero.

They had dug a small hole in the ground. I had to be naked and lying in there. They brought outdoor space heaters up to the location, and they would heat up the hole for ten minutes while setting up the shot. When the camera was ready, I'd have to disrobe, jump in there, and lie down in the snow for a minute or two. Each time, we had to cut because I was shivering and my teeth were chattering uncontrollably. Boy, it was magic. And cold.

The "actors" who were my constant companions in the film were the horse and the hawks. Hawks see about seven times as far as we do, and they can turn their heads 360 degrees. They concentrate very hard, so there is this incredible intensity coming off them. Since the bird was my lover, I always had to take notice of how she was doing. If I was talking to the monk or to the kid and suddenly the hawk would see something while being on my wrist, I would have to incorporate it into my performance. I would take a break and go, "Okay, what's wrong, honey?" Only then could I continue my conversation. The bird was not a prop and I couldn't treat it like one.

We had three birds on the set—one that would sit on my arm, one for flying, and one that wasn't really good for anything. He was also supposed to sit on my arm, but he liked me too much. The moment they put him on my wrist, he would perk up and expand his feathers, which made him look like a chicken. The trainer told me that when some birds feel kind of pleasant, they relax and stick out all their feathers. Of course, it doesn't photograph well for a hawk to look like some chicken—hawks are supposed to look majestic.

"Where's the other bird?" somebody would shout. "This one's not performing well today."

If you've seen the movie, you know that it is very much about the action, and especially the swordplay. A great deal went into staging the sword fights for this movie. Three different types of swords were made for different uses. The steel swords looked the best but were too heavy to really fight with. They were made with hardened steel—steel that is treated with fire, then beaten, then put back in the fire—a process that is hardly known anymore. The heavy hardened steel drains a lot of energy from the person who wields it. It is impossible to initiate blows and then stop them at impact, which is a major technique in the choreography of sword fights. We used the steel swords mostly for close fighting shots.

We also had plastic swords and ones made from titanium composite. Plastic was just for wider shots and looks, and useless and dangerous for fighting because they would break. The titanium version was sweet and light but would also break on occasion. The steel version as well as the titanium would get a nasty swordfish look after too much work, which enabled it to open up any flesh it would connect with—the swords would get little nicks that would become like teeth. The blades would be so screwed up that you could literally saw a piece of wood with them.

The movie's final sword-fight scene is one of the things I'm proud of. Swordplay is not something you do on a daily basis, but I've done it all my life. I think making it seem real is an art. I helped to choreograph the fight scenes, together with the British fight master William Hobbs, who was a genius. We practiced intensely for quite some time on the big fight at the end. In the way you choreograph it, you have to tell a story. The fight is an extension of the characters' being—the way they lose, the way they win, how they do it, what tricks they use, how versatile they are and how gritty, how naughty, how nasty.

They have to be worthy opponents. Of course in a romantic story like this, you know that the hero has to win, so there's a clock ticking there that audiences know about. We found a final move, where the bad guy "finds" his death by falling into Navarre's sword by accident. It was a perfect end. In a sense, it was God's justice.

A small detail I love in the fight is the dagger handling.

Partners in crime. My sister, Machteld, and I were mostly together throughout our childhood.
COURTESY OF THE AUTHOR

Ballet class in acting school, 1965. On the left is a very youthful Jeroen Krabbé. Krabbé played Guus in *Soldier of Orange*. He may be best known in America for playing Dr. Charles Nichols, opposite Harrison Ford, in *The Fugitive*. COURTESY OF THE AUTHOR

With Ineke, the love of my life, in Brussels, Belgium, in 1972.
COURTESY OF THE AUTHOR

In 1970, my best
friend, Marius, died of
Hodgkin's disease at
twenty-nine.
COURTESY OF THE AUTHOR

Shortly after finishing shooting *Soldier of Orange*, 1977. COURTESY OF THE AUTHOR

Sitting next to Jennifer Jason Leigh during a powwow with the cast of *Flesh + Blood*, a medieval film directed by Paul Verhoeven in 1985. Soon after, Jennifer and I would team up again on *The Hitcher*.

COURTESY OF THE AUTHOR

Riding on horseback during the filming of the TV show *Floris* at the dawn of Dutch filmmaking. *Floris* was the first time I teamed up with director Paul Verhoeven (*Basic Instinct, Robocop*) and writer Gerard Soeteman, both of whom I would work with again on *Turkish Delight* and *Soldier of Orange*, the two most popular films in Dutch history. ANP PHOTO/WILLEM VEENMAN

Sylvester Stallone and I square off onboard the Roosevelt Island Tram in one of the more memorable scenes from the 1981 movie *Nighthawks*. In the film, I play the German terrorist, Wulfgar, who has hijacked the tram. Stallone plays Deke DaSilva, the New York City cop bent on stopping me. This was my first American movie, and Stallone and I had problems almost from the start. UNIVERSAL PICTURES/PHOTOFEST

As Wulfgar in *Nighthawks* with a hostage, played by Zoya Leporska. *Nighthawks* was one of the most difficult and demanding experiences of my life. We filmed at night in New York City for two months. Both my mother and my best friend died during the time we were shooting. UNIVERSAL PICTURES/ PHOTOFEST

Director Ridley Scott explains a crucial shot to me on the set of *Blade Runner*.
Ridley's work on *Blade Runner* was a tremendous achievement, and he and I
worked closely together to make Roy Batty "more human than human."

As Roy Batty, being filmed on *Blade Runner*'s neon-drenched Chinatown set.

As vengeful replicant Roy Batty, I chase futuristic detective Rick Deckard (Harrison Ford) onto the ledge of Los Angeles's famed Bradbury Building during the suspenseful climax of *Blade Runner*. COPYRIGHT 1982 WARNER BROTHERS AND THE BLADE RUNNER PARTNERSHIP. COURTESY OF THE PAUL M. SAMMON COLLECTION.

In my greatest role as replicant Roy Batty in *Blade Runner*. Here I catch Deckard just before he falls from a building rooftop during the rain-soaked chase scenes at the end of the movie. Ford was actually suspended from a crane just off-camera. After months of filming, we had to shoot twenty-five hours straight to get these final scenes done. STEPHEN VAUGHAN/MPTV.NET

Here I play the heroic knight, Etienne Navarre, in the 1985 film *Ladyhawke*. It's the story of Navarre and his lover, Isabeau (played by Michelle Pfeiffer), who are the victims of a curse. By day, she is a hawk, and by night, he is a wolf—they are doomed to always be together, yet forever apart. This was a beautiful script based on a medieval story, and I wanted this part very badly. I got it after Kurt Russell dropped out of the movie.
KOBAL/20TH CENTURY FOX/THE KOBAL COLLECTION/WIREIMAGE.COM

A shot of Mickey Rourke and me at the Westwood premiere of *Sin City* on March 28, 2005. Mickey plays Marv, a one-man wrecking crew seeking revenge for the murder of the only woman whom he felt ever loved him. His search leads him to my character—Cardinal Roark. When I arrived in Austin, Texas, for the shoot, we filmed my confrontation with Mickey in an empty room in front of a green screen. Mickey had already done his scenes and left town. MICHAEL CAULFIELD/WIREIMAGE.COM

At one point, Navarre looks up to the tower where one of the guards is about to ring the bell, which was the sign to let the monk know that things had gone wrong. To prevent this, Navarre quickly pulls out a dagger with his left hand because his sword is in his right, flips the dagger in the air, catches it while always keeping an eye on his opponent, and throws it, all in one left-handed move.

BINGO!

It's a skill few actors have, but it is mine. We only had one or two takes for that because we were a bit behind schedule and I was praying that I'd be able to pull it off. I did it in take one and that was it. Navarre kills the guy who is about to ring the bell, but at the same time, the guy dying holds on to the rope, so the bell still tolls. That's good drama and good fun.

I got injured during the fight sequence, setting the schedule back a bit. The concrete studio floor was "carpeted" with a composite of rubber so the horses in the film would not slide too much—a clever safety measure. The rubber pavement looked just like big medieval cobblestones and felt that way as well. The cobblestones did help the horses slide less, but they were rough on our footing. There were uneven stones in there and the boots were not as solid as you might wish for, so I would have too much movement in the boots—the ankles were hardly supported. I sprained an ankle and walked in a cast for ten days before I was able to finish the scene.

I also lost twenty pounds all in that week. My black costume—the color black tends to absorb heat—was handcrafted with about a hundred holes that would lace in the back. It was like a corset. Each of my boots had leather strings, which had to be put through another hundred holes. This would need time and many hands each morning. It would take an hour to get dressed, and once I was strapped in, I was in there for the day. There was no way to get out of the costume—it was pointless to try because getting in and out was two hours work.

The success of this film belongs in no small part to the great director of photography, Vittorio Storaro. He and the crew were Italian. We'd have some funny misunderstandings because Dick Donner couldn't understand what they were talking about—and the Italian crew was always talking. It was hard to get the set quiet.

Before a scene, Dick would shout, "Quiet! Quiet, goddamn it!" But nobody would shut up. So he tried *"Silencio!"* instead. The Italians weren't used to making movies with direct sound—Italian movie sets are notorious for being loud and boisterous affairs, and Dick would feel frustrated by all the noise.

When Storaro was ready, he would say two words to the crew and the whole set would be quiet. Dick would go, "Goddamn it, Rutger. What the hell's going on here?" But Storaro was a magnificent lighting guy and he needed time to get it right.

With Dick's instincts and Storaro's camera work, *Ladyhawke* became not only a beautiful story, but also a very beautiful visual adventure. Grown women and men tell me about the stunning impression *Ladyhawke* made on them more than two decades ago—some of the images in that movie are like laser beams that have burned inside kids' minds for a lifetime.

# CHAPTER 15

## HITCHING A RIDE

*The Hitcher* got hurt one day.

It was 1985, and we were deep in the California desert, just north of the Mexican border. The sandy dunes and the scrub grasses waited with patient anticipation. The sky shimmered, and in the distance the dark ribbon of the two-lane highway seemed to ripple in the baking heat of early afternoon.

I was playing John Ryder, the sinister hitchhiker who spends the entire movie tormenting a young motorist played by C. Thomas Howell. Ryder was a very dark character, described by one reviewer as "a man without a past, without a history, who simply and cruelly hurts and kills people."

As I had done in most of my earlier movies, I did some of my own stunts in *The Hitcher*. That day, we were shooting an action scene where I had to fly through the windshield of the car Tommy Howell was driving. You may recall me in this scene—wearing a long coat, with a large gun in my hand. I needed to hold on to that gun throughout the scene. I also had to finish off the stunt with a tiny bit of the performing art—I actually had to say something. The sequence went like this: cameras rolling, I slide through part of the shattered windshield, land in the passenger seat, turn around, sit up, and, with a slight smile, speak my one-liner.

Something like: "Hi, kid . . . how's it going?"

What could be easier?

Hmm.

We began the sequence, and it progressed well. I flew through the windscreen and landed, all in one piece, in the shotgun seat. Was I okay? I was. Did I still have the gun? I did. Now it was time to say the words—the punch line, the finale of all the action. This was the payoff.

I started speaking. "Hi, kid!"

My lips were already beyond the first words as I sensed a ssslight difference in the way my tongue was trying to pronounce everything.

". . . howsss it going?"

As I got to the end I realized something had changed. Specifically, some piece of my porcelain mouthful was different from how it had been just a moment before. I peeked in the rearview mirror. A front tooth was missing.

The Hitcher was damaged. John Ryder was one villain who needed a complete set of teeth. It is often said that time is money, and nowhere is this more true than on a film set. We were in the middle of the desert, I was missing a tooth, and shooting could not continue. The clock was running, and a lot of people were on that clock. The film company decided to charter a twin-engine airplane to deliver me to a dentist. I was on the plane by the end of the afternoon.

The trip to Santa Monica would take about an hour. I boarded the tiny plane at the military air facility near the small town of El Centro. I had never been in such a nice twin-engine plane before—of course I wanted to sit up front. I squeezed up there with the pilot, settling into the bucket seat, checking out the myriad controls and the wide-open view through the front window. We chatted as we taxied down the runway.

After takeoff, the pilot turned to me. He was a friendly guy, and he gathered from my interest that I knew a little bit about airplanes. "Can you fly one of these?" he said.

I shrugged. "I learned, but I didn't have time to stay on for the license."

He smiled. "Well, let's see what you can do."

He gave me the controls. There was practically nothing to do—these birds are trimmed to do most of the work.

"Take her home," he said when he saw I could handle myself, and he gave me course and altitude. The air was smooth, no turbulence to speak of, with great visibility. We could see for miles. The sun was just dropping to the horizon as we touched down.

They rushed me to a dentist's office near the airport. The temporary missing tooth solution took a few hours, but all went well. Soon enough we were back in the air on our way to El Centro again, except it was night now. The sky was cloudless and dark, with a big, nearly full moon shining almost as bright as the sun. Again the pilot gave me the controls.

The world was a jewel and the plane was in my hands all

the way until just before landing. It was sheer joy. This was my life, and I was a lucky man. If anyone could have seen me I was grinning, flashing my brand-new smile to the world.

\* \* \*

*The Hitcher* was one of those unexpected movies—part thriller, part horror flick—that end up defining a career. It certainly did for me. More than twenty years have passed since we shot it, and yet it stands among the films I've made that keep generating interest long after the fact.

It came about in an unusual way. The director, Robert Harmon, had been a still photographer—he had worked for *Playboy* at one point—and a set photographer for the movies. He decided he wanted to become a director, so he spent more than two years filming and editing a self-financed short film called *China Lake*, which he made with professional actors. Robert intended to use the film as his calling card. *China Lake* was a dark thriller about a serial killer who is also a Los Angeles cop—played by Charles Napier, the square-jawed actor from numerous films and TV shows. During his vacation, the cop rides the lonely desert highways east of L.A. on his police motorcycle, killing random people that he comes across.

While Robert was making that film, a new screenwriter named Eric Red was in Texas finishing a script for a horror story called *The Hitcher*. He had been inspired to write the story because of an old song by The Doors called "Riders on the Storm," part of which is about a hitchhiker who is also a serial killer. In the original script, John Ryder was described as skeletal—more like a monster than a man—and Eric Red once mentioned that he had Rolling Stones guitarist Keith Richards in mind when he wrote the part. He also felt that Ryder should have no natural voice—he should have an electronic voice box like a throat-cancer survivor.

Both projects landed on the desk of producer Ed Feldman around the same time. Feldman could hardly miss the coincidence that *China Lake* had the same look and feel implied by *The Hitcher,* and practically the same story, so he married script and director. They hired C. Thomas Howell from *E.T.* to play the kid. They went through several possible actors while looking for the man to play John Ryder—and settled on Sam Elliott. Apparently, Elliott was so scary when he came in to audition that Ed Feldman was afraid to go out to his car afterward. But Elliott had a scheduling conflict, and shortly afterward he had to back out of the role.

As this was going on, I was finishing my publicity appearances for *Ladyhawke,* and I was in Los Angeles. When *The Hitcher* script came to me, I was blown away. It was written so tight—not a wasted word in the entire movie. Then I met with Robert and he screened *China Lake* for me. It was beautiful.

In those days, I was still reluctant to take the whole job as an actor for real. It's important to remember that I was not a star—I was nobody. I had been a star in Holland, but Holland is a small country. I had been working in the United States since 1980, and I still felt like I wasn't going to make it as an English-language actor, or as any kind of actor. Until *Ladyhawke,* the movies I had made in the States had not been hits. My career could have ended at any time, and I was prepared for that to happen.

Before I took the part, some people in the press were saying to me that after *Ladyhawke,* I should stick with the heroic characters and romantic leading men. I had a moment there where I thought they were right, and that was depressing—above all, I am an actor. All the same, I felt that this was a very playful bad guy. The role had depth—it wasn't going to be a cliché with one dimension. It was going to be a man without hope or love or any human touches. It took me thirty seconds to make up my mind—I decided to go for it.

The story involves a young man named Jim Halsey who is driving along a desert highway in Texas in the middle of the night. He picks up a lone hitchhiker, my character, John Ryder. Very soon, Ryder reveals that he is a murderer, and he challenges Halsey to stop him from killing again. What follows is a cat-and-mouse game across the desert as a weird bond grows between the two men.

The movie reels from one haunting battle to the next, with numerous bystanders, including cops, ending up dead. Along the way, Halsey meets a love interest, Nash, played by Jennifer Jason Leigh. Ryder reserves a final and particularly grisly fate for Nash. In the end, Halsey and Ryder have it out on a stretch of highway, and Halsey guns Ryder down—the fate Ryder has been asking for all along.

My take on Ryder was that he knows he's "troubled," but he doesn't know how to get fixed. He wants to die, but he doesn't have the guts to kill himself. It would really be best if somebody came along and said, "You need to die now and I'm going to do it for you." When he hooks up with the kid he gets a feeling about him—maybe this is the guy—and it makes him all warm inside.

When I first met C. Thomas Howell on the set, he was excited. He had been a successful child and teen actor, had recently turned eighteen years old, and he wasn't entirely happy with the work he had done in the past. He said, "You know, I've never really acted before. This is going to be my first time."

Tommy has spent twenty years telling people that dealing with me on that set was some sort of life-altering experience. He has said that he found me frightening, intimidating, and that he was in a constant state of fear, almost as if he really was Jim Halsey and I really was John Ryder.

He and I did a movie together in South Africa in 2004, and even then, he told me he still had some of these feelings left over from *The Hitcher*.

All I could say was "For Christ's sake, why didn't you tell me?"

I was on the set that whole shoot, behaving normally, joking around with people, and jumping into character just before we did our takes—pretty much like I always do. I was a professional actor playing my role as well as I could. I was available to talk with him at any time about what we were doing—and would have been happy to do so. I never had any idea that he was afraid of me—we would meet on the set and he would act very friendly. Then we would do the scene and he would seem genuinely frightened, but I thought it was because he was acting well—really going with his part and with what was happening.

It's a funny coincidence that Jennifer Jason Leigh came to be in this movie with us—I had only just finished shooting a movie called *Flesh + Blood* with her in Spain. Now I was on the set of *The Hitcher* and we were ready to go, but we didn't have anyone to play the part of Nash. Originally, it was a small role that came toward the end of the movie. I didn't know where they were looking or what they intended to do about it. Then one day they said, "We'll have a scene with the girl tomorrow—we found her and she's coming in."

"So who is it?"

When they told me it was Jennifer, I thought that was out of sight. I didn't have much with her on *The Hitcher*, but I had a lot with her on *Flesh + Blood*, which was a medieval drama we did with Paul Verhoeven directing—Paul's first English-language film. Jennifer is a great actress—she dives right into a role, she's smart, and she's great to work with. I felt at home with her right away, from the moment I met her.

Our one scene together in *The Hitcher* takes place near the end. In that scene, Nash and Jim Halsey are hiding out in a motel room, but Ryder has followed them there. Halsey goes into the bathroom and takes a shower, leaving Nash dozing on the bed. Ryder comes in and lies down next to her. He looks at her longingly and sort of pets her. It was a moment that I asked Robert Harmon to put in there.

As it was written, Ryder basically comes in, gets on the bed, and grabs her. I asked for the longer scene because I had this idea that Ryder has a form of amnesia—he's looking at Nash like he can almost remember what love was, he just can't remember when. I had that same feeling about him when he slips the dismembered finger into Halsey's french fries. Ryder has this sideline activity where he cuts people up, but he never really remembers doing it. He feels like "Sure, I know that happened, but it wasn't me. It must have been somebody else."

The next thing that happens to Nash in the movie is also something I asked for. The script called for Ryder to pin Nash to a wall with his pickup truck. When Halsey gets there, Ryder says, "Okay, you have to kill me now. If you don't kill me, I'm going to kill your girl."

I said to Robert, "Can we up the stakes here? Wouldn't it be great if he had somehow gotten hold of a tractor trailer instead of a pickup?" Robert and I were on the same page for most of this movie, so he was right there with me. I think the truck makes the scene more weighty and more extreme. Just the sound of it revving makes people go, "Oh, boy. That's really horrible."

One other thing I asked Robert for: There's a scene where Ryder comes crashing through the wall of a gas station in a pickup truck, spins the truck around, and crashes through the gas pumps, all while Halsey looks on in terror. The trick there was the stuntmen had to slide the truck around and bring it back so it would be positioned for the camera. After a few tries, none of them could seem to do it.

"Robert," I said, "I know I can do this."

Before I became a film actor in Holland, I spent quite a bit of time with cars. I took courses in dirt-track racing, in racing on hard surfaces, in sliding the car and doing spins. I even studied dirt-bike racing to prepare for a role as a motorcycle racer in a Dutch film called *Spetters*. Robert did give me the chance, and I nailed the stunt in one take.

All of these highway scenes were shot on location, and the locations themselves were painstakingly researched and picked by Robert Harmon and his director of photography, John Seale. Both Robert and John are excellent photographers, and John would go on to win an Oscar for his camera work in *The English Patient*. I rented a motor home for the length of the shoot, and I ended up sleeping in it many nights—I put about six thousand miles on it during the six weeks we were in the desert.

People say this movie is scary—so much so that most people miss out on how much humor there is until they've seen it two or three times. The Ryder character has a certain charm and a certain joie de vivre. We don't know where it comes from, but we don't have to know. It's just that he's winking to the audience, and he continues to do so throughout the movie. I think that if you push the fear button with people during the first thirty minutes, they're often paralyzed by that, and it takes some time for it to wear off and for people to go, "Oh, there's something fun going on here."

When I was making this movie, I had a fairy tale in the back of my mind. It's a tiny fairy tale that I remember from my childhood. It's about a guy who was taught to be fearless. It goes like this:

Once upon a time, there was a guy who wanted to know what fear was, so he went out into the world and he traveled and traveled, and he didn't find it. By the end of the day, he was really tired and he found this castle and he knocked on the door.

A beautiful girl opened the door, and said, "What are you doing?"

The guy said, "I'm tired now, but I'm looking for fear. I haven't found it today, but maybe tomorrow."

"Don't worry about it," the girl said. "Come inside, go to sleep, and then tomorrow will be another day."

In the middle of the night, the girl entered his room with a bucket of live sardines. At the stroke of midnight, she poured the sardines over his stomach while he was asleep. He woke up with a start and now he knew fear.

It's a fairy tale by Grimm, and a weird little story, but in the back of my mind, that was *The Hitcher*—the phantom who shows up and does all kinds of tricks that teach the guy to overcome his fear, and challenges him to see if he can get beyond it. But in order to get there, the kid has to kill the hitcher.

"Here are the bullets for the gun. Here's the gun—you can shoot me now." After crossing that line, there's another life waiting, but the kid is still just a kid and he's not ready. He goes, "You're crazy. I won't do it."

And the hitcher thinks, "Well, okay. I'll try again. I'll come back later."

# CHAPTER 16

## THE LEGENDARY ERMANNO

During the 1980s, an Italian man named Ermanno Olmi became ill and took to his bed, where he remained for two years. Nobody knew exactly what his problem was—doctors couldn't figure it out. He had lost his equilibrium, was not able to walk, and was in danger of falling over whenever he stood up.

None of this would have made much difference to my life, except that Ermanno Olmi is one of the best directors. His epic film, *The Tree of the Wooden Clogs,* is on many lists as one of the greatest movies ever made. He is a giant.

One morning, he got out of bed and began to go through the normal routine that he had abandoned two years before.

People who saw him said, "Ermanno! What are you doing out of bed?"

"I've had an idea. I'm going to make a movie—*The Legend of the Holy Drinker*. And what's more, I'm going to do it in the English language, and film it in Paris."

He started to put together plans for the movie. Now, Ermanno has never worked like most other directors. He would do everything himself—that was his way. He would operate the camera, and usually, he didn't like to work with professional actors. To play his characters, he would cast real people that he spotted on the street. On *The Legend of the Holy Drinker*, he felt that he needed at least one actor, for the main role.

Around that time, I was touring Europe, doing TV and newspaper interviews to promote *The Hitcher*. One day, he saw me on television. He hadn't found an actor for his lead role yet. He turned to his assistant and said, "That's the man I want. That man there, on the TV."

"The hitcher?"

"Yes. Him."

I was speaking English in the interview he saw, and he didn't speak a word of English. They were translating what I said into Italian. What's even stranger is that he had no idea who I was. He just had a feeling. When they approached me with this intriguing offer, I couldn't resist meeting him. By the time we sat down together sometime later, he had watched a few of my movies.

In the story, I play Andreas, a guy who is an out-of-work, homeless Polish man in Paris. He is an alcoholic. One day, he meets a man who offers him a great gift—two hundred francs. Andreas is too proud to accept money he knows he can never repay, but the man tells him not to worry. He doesn't want to be repaid. What he does want is that if Andreas ever has the chance he should return the money to the statue of St. Therese de Lisieux in a nearby church.

Andreas agrees, and spends the rest of the movie trying to keep his promise. What follows is Andreas's quest—a quest complicated by the appearance of the spirits of dead friends and by Andreas's own penchant for liquor and temptation. He's in a constant state of wide-eyed wonder, not understanding why things are happening this way, and why they're happening now. It's starting to dawn on him that maybe God has a purpose for him, and that there is a reason for these people showing up.

He starts to believe he is becoming part of a miracle, but basically he is a guy who drinks himself to death and doesn't really know it. The film is based on a novel by the German writer Joseph Roth, who died an alcoholic in Paris in 1939—the story is considered his spiritual testament.

The end of the story is quite endearing. Andreas has lost the money, but then he gets it back. In his last moment, he has one last drink in a café. Then he has a heart attack, and he doesn't quite get the money to the church. The people carry him, because they don't want the dead guy to lie in the café. They go, "Why don't we bring him over to the church? It's better there." So they drag him across the square and he ends up sitting in the church with the money. It's still stuck between his fingers, his debt paid.

In doing this film, Ermanno and I crossed quite a few bridges together. We had to work through a translator. The first translator was too young to really understand what we were talking about—she was in her twenties and this story was way before her time. We had to fire her and get a more mature person. Meanwhile, we were transforming a German story into an English-language film. If we had a conflict about the story, we both would go back to the German version of the book.

Everything on the set was strange. Some people were so peculiar, real alcoholics, street people who were living in the same hotel we were shooting in. They were playing what they were actually living, and they were giving their best. Ermanno was great with them—they forgot they were acting and became the most beautiful part of themselves. They were moving like trees in dreams.

My relationship with Ermanno couldn't have been better. Even now, I feel close to him in many ways. One of the first things he said to me was "It's an action movie." Then he pointed to his heart and my face. "But the action is all here." Then he said, "I'm looking for a little Peter Sellers from *Being There* and a little Charlie Chaplin." Of course, Charlie Chaplin had a funny way of moving and doing things, and Peter Sellers was brilliant as Chauncey Gardener, the man who has all the wisdom, but at the same time has no idea what's going on. Or did he?

I've met a few who drink all the time. It has nothing to do with holding a glass or a bottle. The thing is, every time someone plays an alcoholic, they seem to overplay it—the bottle is never out of their hand and they play some sort of stumble-bum. We didn't want that. We said let's create a drunk, but we don't want to show all these bottles—we need to see it now and then, but not always. So we have this little scene. After a long night of drinking, Andreas is sleeping under a bridge, and he has some newspapers around him. He wakes up and rolls over. There's a bottle behind him, and he sets it in motion—the bottle starts rolling over the cobblestones down to the river. Simple, sweet.

There is a moment in this part of the movie that I love. In the scene I just described, Andreas is waking up in the morning, after he has received the money from the stranger. So he wakes up and goes, "What did I do last night?" He realizes that he ate and drank for the first time in a long time. He counts his money, and as he does, in the background there are two sleeping homeless guys that really lived there under the bridge.

Before we did this scene, I said, "In the scene under the bridge, can there be a dog somehow? Let's have one dog."

They said, "You want a dog? What for?"

"I don't know. Let's just have a dog. Okay? Any kind of dog." If I have an idea that sort of holds me, I find that it almost always works, somehow.

They tried to get a dog, but it didn't happen. They said, "We don't have the dog. It didn't come yet." So I shot the scene without the dog, and I wasn't in the next scene. Then the dog arrived.

The next shot was just two beggars waking up, and one of them eats a piece of bread, and that's it. I said to Ermanno, "Listen, please believe me. Put the dog in the scene. It doesn't matter what the dog does. Just put it in the scene."

Ermanno said, "Okay. I'll try it."

Then I went home to my hotel room. I was done for the day. I didn't know if he used the dog, but when I saw the movie, there's a scene between these two real homeless guys. They have a little moment. Then the dog walks into the shot. He walks up to one of them and smells in his mouth. It almost looks like the dog's kissing him. Maybe it's not a big deal, but it made that scene. And because the dog wasn't in time for my scene, the dog now walks into the other scene and makes it amazing. It's beautiful.

*Legend of the Holy Drinker* is a hard movie to find in the United States. My challenge was to see if I could help bring the story into the American market—it didn't quite happen, not in the way we hoped. The film did become a big success in Europe, however, and it won several awards. Ermanno won the 1988 Venice Film Festival Award for Best Director. The movie also won the 1989 David of Donatello Award for Best Film. For my part, I won the 1988 Seattle International Film Festival Award for Best Actor.

As an actor, sometimes you are looking for something and you have only a vague feeling about it. You would like to express something, but you can't put it into words. They ask you what kind of film you would like to do, and you're going, "Well, it has to do about love—love and harder passion. It has to do with sensitivity and truthfulness and good faith and gentleness." That doesn't make sense to anyone, but you can't really explain it any better. Then, sometimes you meet a brilliant person, who sees things that everyone else seems to miss, and he or she tells you what it is you're looking for. When you work with that person it's like you're dancing on your toes. You work twice as hard as ever, and you're flying—that's what it was like to work with Ermanno.

# CHAPTER 17

## THE BLIND LEADING THE BLOND

I was on a roll.

On the heels of *Ladyhawke*, *The Hitcher*, and *The Legend of the Holy Drinker*, I was in a period I think of as my "Prime Time." I was making movies, and they were all very different sorts of roles. I was making money, was higher on the list, and by the end of the decade, I had finally moved to Los Angeles full-time. Of course, I was still the same actor, but like a butcher, over time you gain more precision in the way you cut the meat. For my next movie, I cut the meat with a samurai sword.

In *Blind Fury*, I play Nick Parker, a blind samurai. An American soldier in Vietnam, he loses his sight in an explosion and goes missing in action. Local villagers save him and nurse him back to health. They teach him martial arts, and he becomes adept at using his very blindness as a snare to lull his enemies into a false sense of security. He also becomes a master at sword fighting, using the blade he keeps hidden inside his cane.

Back in the United States, he goes to visit an old army buddy in Miami, only to find the man has divorced and moved to Reno, Nevada. During his visit with his friend's ex-wife, the house is attacked by thugs trying to kidnap the man's nine-year-old son. Unknown to Parker, his friend is involved in the drug trade. Parker thwarts the kidnap attempt, but the boy's mother is shot in the struggle. With her dying breath, she begs Parker to take the boy safely to his father. Thus begins a dangerous, cross-country journey as Parker must constantly fight off attackers in his quest to reunite father and son.

*Blind Fury* was one of the most challenging and exciting jobs for me because of the training involved. It's one thing to learn to use a sword, another to learn to act like a blind man, and quite another to do both at the same time. I trained for a month with Lynn Manning, a blind man who is also a judoka—an expert in judo. He taught me what it was like to have his handicap, and how to walk and move like a blind man. Then he came onto the set with us in Reno, Nevada, to answer any more questions that might arise.

Lynn was a wonderful guy and an inspiration to be around. He was tall—taller than me—with a great sense of humor and a lot of energy. He had lost his eyesight as an adult—he had been working with juveniles in Los Angeles and one of the kids shot him in the head. Lynn survived the gunshot, but never saw again. Regardless, it didn't slow him down much or put a damper on his enthusiasm.

One of the actors on the shoot was an ex-professional boxer, Randall "Tex" Cobb, who played one of the bad guys. Cobb was famous for having a rock-solid chin—he once fought Larry Holmes for the heavyweight championship and lasted all fifteen rounds despite getting pummeled from beginning to end. He had aged out of boxing and now was doing some acting—he had earlier played the bounty hunter in *Raising Arizona*.

Tex Cobb and Lynn had this same wickedness to them. They were two very bright men who would argue for hours in the hotel bar about philosophy and the meaning of life—all the while drinking their asses off. They agreed on just about nothing, and yet they loved each other's company, probably because they were both fighters.

The day I met Lynn, he was getting ready for a world-championship judo tournament for the visually impaired that was to take place in Seoul, South Korea. I went to the place in Los Angeles where he was practicing. Moments after we were introduced, he said to me, "So, have you done any martial-arts training?"

"Well, yeah. You know—a little bit."

He gestured toward the mat and smiled. "Do you want to play?"

"Why not?"

We got out there and he had me pinned to the floor in about twenty seconds. It was no contest. In fact, I was so charmed by him and by his abilities that I decided to become one of his sponsors for the Seoul games. He didn't win the tournament, but he did quite well, advancing several rounds.

One of the first things that he did in our training together was to take me around the block blindfolded. "I have an advantage," he said. "I don't get confused about what I see—my eyes don't play tricks on me." His intention was to show me what the world outside was like to a blind man—how lost you can get and how sharp your hearing becomes. We made quite a pair getting ready for that little walk—he was blind and I was blindfolded.

"Okay," he said, "let's go to the street." As we started walking, I quickly got disoriented. I started sweating and was nearly in a panic—the traffic was just to our right. Meanwhile, he was calm as he pointed out the things in the street that would help him navigate—basically, things that he could hear. The man had the most incredible hearing—his ears had become his eyes. He could literally hear, in a room full of people, if somebody was upset just by the sound of their breathing.

When we flew from Los Angeles to Reno, there was some talk on the plane that it would snow later that day. And Lynn, who'd never really been out of Los Angeles before he lost his sight, said, "You know? I've never seen snow." By the time we arrived at the hotel, it had started snowing, and he was ecstatic. It kept snowing really heavily, and after dinner, he said, "I want to see how it is and feel it."

A bunch of us went outside to the pool area. There were several inches of snow already on the ground, and we all started throwing snowballs. Lynn and I were across the covered pool from each other, and I heard him call out.

"Rutger?!?"

"Yeah?" I said. "What?" As I turned to look at him, I got

pelted by a snowball he had thrown. Just by hearing my voice, he instantly found my location, and he nailed me.

Lynn was quite a character. It was April when we got to Reno, so the winter was ending, and he got the idea in his head that he would like to go skiing before it did.

"Come on, Rutger. What do you say?"

"I say you've got to be fucking kidding me."

"No, no. I'm serious. I want to go skiing. I've never done it before and now's the time."

The next day was a Sunday, and also the last day of the ski season. We went to a little ski mountain—it was snowing that day, but it was pretty warm and conditions were slow. You wouldn't call it the ideal ski day, but given our circumstances, it was probably what we were looking for. In those days, I used to have a friend, a cameraman named Bill Bristow, accompany me on my films—he would make behind-the-scenes documentaries of the movie shoots. Bill was all for this ski outing, so the three of us went together. We rented equipment, and we all got on the ski lift.

The plan was that we would keep Lynn between Bill and me, go slow, and make sure nobody got killed. I would be in front, then it would be Lynn, and then it would be Bill, three sets of skis snowplowing down the hill. We would keep him in check all the time so he wouldn't veer off on his own.

As we took off down the hill, I was already sweating like a pig. I was nervous because I felt responsible if something should happen to Lynn. At the same time, I was about to start filming a movie and I wasn't supposed to be doing anything like skiing.

"Oh, this is great," Lynn was saying behind me. "I love this. This is great."

We came down the hill very slowly and very smoothly and he was having a ball with it. We crashed a few times but nothing serious. Then we were almost done; we were five hundred feet from the lodge and a cup of hot coffee, and it was the last stretch, a very mild slope about forty feet wide. I was on Lynn's left, and Bill was on his right. Everything was fine and we were calm. Lynn had already learned enough that he was going on his own, and we let him get out ahead of us a little bit.

Off to the right, the track branched off and the slope became quite steep. It headed toward some kind of ravine. You wouldn't want to go there and Lynn started moving in that direction. He was going faster now, and he started pulling away from us.

"Hey, Lynn! Don't go over there!"

"Over where?" he said.

"Oh shit! Go to the left! Go to the left! Put your weight on the right ski. STOP!"

Things went south very rapidly—in a matter of a few seconds. He didn't know what to do and he kept going to the right. We sped up but he was too far ahead. He headed straight for the drop-off, gathering momentum. If he went off he would fall and hit a lot of naked gravel with no warning and no chance to prepare himself.

The two of us accelerated. We crashed into Lynn and grabbed him right as he went over the edge. We all ended up on our bellies in a sort of pile, with Lynn's upper body hanging off the side while he laughed like a madman.

"Jesus Christ!" I said.

We were holding on to him, trying to get him up, but we were giggling so hard that it took a long, long time.

I think of *Blind Fury* as my best action movie, and it was the fittest I had ever been for any movie—but it also became my last real action movie. Prior to filming, and during the entire seven weeks of the shoot, I worked out an hour and a half every morning to maintain my ability to take the strain. I was playing a blind Vietnam vet who had some serious hand-to-hand combat—physicality was a big part of the role.

I had always been an action actor, yet even as I worked out, for the first time I realized that things were changing for me. As the *Blind Fury* shoot progressed, I knew it was time to see if I could start doing more movies that were not totally action. It scared me a little because that's a bridge not easily taken, but in the meantime, we were having fun. I had a ball working with the director Philip Noyce, with Meg Foster, whom I had worked with before in *The Osterman Weekend*, and with Brandon Call, who played the young kid Billy. We made a warm, playful, and lighthearted movie. Being so physical, however, it wasn't without its scary moments.

I remember a scene we had where I was on top of a mountain, in a station where a cable car would come in. We were outside on a veranda of sorts, and I had to fight a few guys there. For the wide shot, they were using a stuntman to play me, and I was just having a good time watching them film—the cable car had brought us up, and we all had to wait there until the scene was done. While I watched them rehearse I thought, "There's something here I don't like."

It was not a difficult stunt. It was a guy going over the railing of the veranda, just like in the old cowboy movies. My stunt double hits him, he goes over the railing, and he falls. About ten feet below the veranda, they had piled a bunch of cardboard boxes for him to fall on, which is a normal setup. But next to the pile I noticed there was a steel pipe sticking out of the wall. It was pretty far out of the line of his fall, but if he did happen to fall that way, it wouldn't be very good. I mentioned this to the stunt guys, but they pooh-poohed it.

I said to Bill Bristow, "Bill, you film this for me because I feel really weird."

Sure enough, something went wrong in the fight. The guy slipped and went too far to the right, hitting that pipe head-first, just above his eye. The impact knocked him for a loop, but he was okay a little while later, and he was lucky not to lose the eye.

For me, the last fight scene in the movie is the most special part, and it took place after shooting was over. When we first shot the film, we did it without an actual sword fight. As they started to edit it, they realized that I went through the whole movie with this sword hidden in my walking stick, and there was really no payoff to it. But then I went to Australia to shoot a film called *Salute of the Jugger,* and I was gone for two months. When I returned, they called me.

"Rutger, will you come back in?"

"Sure, what's the problem?"

"The ending is kind of weak, and we need to do something with that sword you carry the whole time."

"Sounds like fun."

They brought in an actor and martial artist named Sho Kosugi, who is a master swordsman. He had been in *Enter the Ninja* and many other movies. The idea was that after I had dispatched all of the bad guys, he would appear and we would have one last battle that would take us all over the room and along the edge of a hot tub. I met with Kosugi and we trained together. He was delighted by this role because he could finally do a sword fight without being a samurai or a ninja. He said, "I've done fifty movies and nobody's ever seen my face before. I've always had to wear a mask."

Our period of preparation was short—maybe a week—and I really didn't think I could handle the scene. Kosugi was very supportive, always saying "You're going to be fine. You can do this." We ended up doing a very funny, tongue-in-cheek sort of scene, a little bit like Jackie Chan is famous for.

*Blind Fury* did relatively well in terms of making money, and there was some talk of making several of these Nick Parker movies. The story was adapted from a series of old Japanese samurai stories, so there was a lot to work with, and the studio felt they could handle doing more. It had the classic ending where the hero, the blind samurai, walks off into the distance, to reappear somewhere else at another time. I had never done a sequel before, but Nick was a lovely character and I would've considered it in this case. Unfortunately, the idea never quite got off the ground.

# CHAPTER 18

## WANDERING IN THE DESERT

Life is an adventure. You can die anytime.

In 1989, I was deep in the Australian Outback, shooting *Salute of the Jugger,* which in some places was called *The Blood of Heroes*. It was a strange film, written and directed by David Webb Peoples, one of the writers of *Blade Runner,* and the man who would also write Clint Eastwood's *The Unforgiven*. It was David's debut as a director. In a post-apocalyptic, *Mad Max*-type world, human survivors live in isolated settlements, scraping a desperate living from the barren earth. Life is bleak, unrelenting toil, with no way to gain pleasure or escape—save one. Teams of *juggers* wander the wasteland, playing a savage blood sport that delights the crowds, but leaves its combatants scarred and, often, dead. My character, Sallow, leads a team from settlement to settlement, taking on and defeating all juggers.

Sallow was interesting to me because he was so cold. To me, this was almost an avant-garde film because the language is filed down to the most basic level—nobody wastes words, nobody says, "How are you?" In this empty world, there is no original language left.

We shot in Australia for two months; we were out in the desert for half that time, and the desert is incredible. It's vast, it's amazing, and it's seductive in a dangerous way. I had arranged to take an off-road motorcycle with me on location. So one day while we were working, lunchtime came and I felt like going for a ride. I thought, "I've got half an hour. I'll be back before anybody misses me." I sort of just crept away. In full costume, I wheeled the motorcycle to the edge of the set location, hopped on, and took off. I was a forty-five-year-old man, being just a little bit naughty.

I started cruising around a little bit, not going too far from the encampment. The first really weird thing I noticed was that they have these bushes and they look sweet and romantic. They're actually stone. So I tore open my pants on one of the bushes because I thought it was a plant. I hit it, but just slightly. It took part of my skin off and now my leg was bleeding.

Then I came around this corner and on a little slope there was this enormous kangaroo lying like a girl tanning in the sun. It was literally lying there like Marilyn Monroe, its arms up over its head. It had this big long face. It looked at me like, "Oh shit. Here's another human idiot."

I stopped the bike, going "What the . . . ?" I'd never before met a kangaroo in the flesh.

The kangaroo got up slowly, like he was bored, and must have been nine feet tall. He gave me one more long, annoyed look and started hopping away. I was watching this and I thought, "I wonder how fast this guy goes?"

I started following him, and now he started leaping. These were really relaxed leaps, but he was making good progress. Because of the terrain, I had to make little bends and turns around rocks and plants and little hills. And he was just leaping along, going *Thonk, thonk, thonk.* I'd say every jump was at least twenty feet. He was practically flying, in that relaxed way of his, and I was not keeping up. At some point, he was too far ahead and I decided to abandon the race.

That's where things got funny. I sat there on the bike, and thoughts crossed my mind. I'm in the middle of the desert. I'm three thousand miles away from Sydney. The big afternoon sun is right there in the sky—there's no shadow other than the one beneath me—and I didn't bring any water. I had zigzagged around, and now I thought, "What direction did I take?"

I turned around, but I didn't see the film-crew encampment. I didn't see it on any horizon. There were no roads that I could see. I didn't see anything but empty land, shimmering in the heat. I was totally lost in the desert in less than ten minutes.

"Jesus, this is not a good thing."

I started cruising a little bit this way, and a little bit that way.

Left or right? I'm not sure. I'm sure it gets quite unhealthy if you pick the wrong way. People die in the desert—especially people who do things like chase after kangaroos. It happens. But I am not panicking. Not yet. I am shitting my pants, but not panicking.

I make a choice—I go right. I follow a track along for about four minutes, I come over the top of the hill, and there's the set, laid out like a small town below me. Lunch is just about over.

And how happy I am to be alive.

*       *       *

The 1990s were dawning by the time *Salute of the Jugger* came out—a decade when I worked on a lot of projects.

It was during this time that I appeared in the TV commercials for Guinness Beer. These advertisements, which people in England loved, and people in Ireland loathed, were some of the first absurd TV commercials. In them, I played the Pure Genius, a dark and mysterious pitchman who explored topics like physics, the subconscious, time and eternity—all in a playful and ironic way. The job came to me because they were looking for some blond guy to do a couple of commercials— maybe two or three over the course of a year. But they proved so popular in England that through the early 1990s, we made more than twenty of these things.

We had several different directors, including *Blade Runner's* Ridley Scott, who had been a longtime director of television commercials before he got into feature filmmaking. He was one of the best in that field, and it was a pleasure to work with him again. The commercials themselves were wonderful fun, real pop art that I was proud to have my hand in. Each director put their own spin on it, and I'm told that the first ads jump-started a 22 percent increase in Guinness sales.

However, one of my favorite filmmaking experiences acting on a motorcycle was a movie called *Surviving the Game*. In that film, a young homeless man, Jack Mason—played by the rapper-turned-actor Ice-T—is persuaded by a group of hunters to work for them on a Pacific Northwest expedition. Only after he has traveled with them to a remote wilderness location does he discover that he won't actually be working for them—he's going to be their prey.

Six sportsmen take part in the hunt. They include former CIA operatives who do it as recreation, a guy whose wife and child have been murdered and wants to take his revenge on somebody—anybody—and a Wall Street tycoon who brings along his reluctant son as a rite of manhood. Cut loose in the wilderness with a brief head start, streetwise Mason proves surprisingly resourceful, turning the tables on his pursuers—who are on four-wheeled motorcycles and are armed with high-powered rifles—in a deadly game of cat and mouse. In the film, I play Burns, the evil travel agent and tour operator who makes his living organizing these hunts.

The story of *Surviving the Game* is not new. It's based on an older story called "The Most Dangerous Game," and the idea has been done in film and on television several times. What a nasty and vicious tale—they choose a homeless man because no one will miss him, and anyone who did would never be believed. I found this story to be one of the most cruel that I've done. It's fascinating to work on such cynical material, and I took great pleasure trying to make the character as sinister as possible.

The director of this movie was Ernest Dickerson, who was the director of photography on some of Spike Lee's films. In my talks with Ernest, I was able to convince him—small detail as it may be—that in the chase scenes, Burns should ride a motocross bike rather than a four-wheeler. It gave him his "brand" in wider shots and created a visual sense that Burns was the leader of the pack. It also gave me the chance to ride the Kawasaki twin-cylinder 650, which is a bike I have owned and love to ride. The bike reminded me of knights on horseback, and Burns becomes a bit of a dark knight while riding it.

I added a lot of detail to the Burns character. I made him wear glasses, which suggests that he has a vulnerable side. He is a quick thinker. In a weird way he is a family man to his hunters and he cooks their dinner. He has a taste for the good things in life—he drinks expensive wine. He plays chess. He has a talking parrot to keep him company in his office. He has a love for exotic butterflies—dead, of course—and great love for nature's seasons and laws.

He also has a deep bitterness toward the pathetic human race. Of course, the big surprise is that the poor homeless man outwits the hunters and begins to kill them off. This is a lovely blind side which Burns doesn't anticipate, but even then he still likes the game—he doesn't mind seeing his clients die. Only when Mason manages to kill his partner Cole do things turn more serious for Burns.

I felt that Burns should be like a father to his hunters. My whole take was that he doesn't show off, he lets the kids play, but when they get out of line, he has to put the shock to them, intimidate them, and say, "These are the rules, this is the game, and you obey me." He needed a sense of respect from these men, and my challenge was to have Burns control them with his mind—by cleverness and dark power. I had nice moments where I put the psychological screws to each of the hunters in turn.

The time came when I had done all of the hunters except one—a deranged psychiatrist played by the veteran actor Gary Busey. My scene came with him when we were shooting a dinner party. The whole group is at the cabin, and they have a nice dinner. It's their last night together, and in the morning they're going to start the game. The victim doesn't even know what's going on yet—he's like the lamb here. So the idea is that Gary acts up at the table, he gets a little bit out of line, and I have to say, "Look, just don't forget, here's the deal. You know the rules here, right? Do you understand? Do you agree? Good."

We started rehearsing the dinner scene, we were behind schedule, and we knew we weren't going to get it in that day. Then Gary showed up with this two-page monologue he had written for himself, which he wanted to add to the scene. It was about how when his character was a child, his father made him kill his favorite dog, George Henry Stout. Gary is a guy with a lot of manic energy, and he was especially up for this shoot. He said, "I rewrote some of this stuff and I want to see how you like it."

The story he wrote was a bit long, and a bit crazy, and there was a lot of drama and poetry to it. He launched into it and the rest of us were sitting around the table, going, "Okay, uh . . . When is he going to finish?" Dinner-table scenes are hard to get through in the best case—there's not much happening and it's not easy to keep them moving. Now Gary was doing this crazy story, and the director's going "Hmm. Interesting. Okay, let's try it."

As we rehearsed, Gary was basically running around the table, getting into everybody's shots. Anytime someone had something to say, the moment they were going to say it, Gary Busey was there in the shot going "Hey, how're you doing? How're you doing?" He was all over the place and in the middle of the scene he had this long monologue, so now he's imagined the dinner party as a big vehicle for himself. This isn't all that out of the ordinary—movie acting is often a subtle competition to see who's going to win the scene, but the key word is *subtle*. It isn't usually this over-the-top.

At the end of his story, I'm supposed to pull him by the tie and say, "Look, that's all really interesting, but cut the crap and obey the rules." But Gary is a guy who never quite sits still— he's always moving around—and when we rehearsed our little chat, I felt like it didn't go the way the story intended. I didn't get to corner him and I really didn't rein him in much at all. He was blowing me off, going "Yeah, sure. Whatever." On top of that, he may have been using some serious drugs.

I went home that night thinking "What can I as a character do to put this guy in his place? What can I do to get his attention?" I didn't sleep much because I wanted to find something and I couldn't come up with it.

The next day we shot the scene. It went along okay and everybody got their moment. Gary got his monologue and it was amazing. And for the last shot, we still had his close-up as I tell him, "Look, that's all well and good, but you're still gonna get fucked up if you screw with my rules."

We were about to do this close-up, and suddenly it dawned

on me how to get him. I took the director aside and said, "I think I can get something special out of him. If it doesn't work, we'll try something else." He was fine with it.

Now, when a person does his close-up, you're there with him, feeding him your lines from off camera. You try to do your lines the same way as you would while you're being filmed—or with some small variation. So Gary was expecting me to say my lines the same way as always.

The camera was on him and I said, "John fucking Henry Stout." Nowhere was it in my lines to talk about his dog, and for a few long seconds I could see Gary thinking a hundred miles an hour. His eyes went wider and wilder than before, and he had no idea what I was implying. He actually looked cornered, his eyeballs moving back and forth—it was beautiful. So I took my time and then delivered my last lines. "Obey the rules!"

My favorite moment in this film comes near the end. By then, nearly all of the hunters are dead. The only people still alive are the Wall Street financier played by F. Murray Abraham from *Amadeus*; Ice-T's character, Mason; and my character, Burns. The financier has lost his son in the fighting, and has now gone berserk. In the middle of the night, he and Mason have it out—a final dogfight. Rather than join in, Burns decides to wait it out and see who wins.

There was a consultant on the shoot who was a commando and a Vietnam vet. He was there to teach us some combat techniques. While he and I were talking he mentioned that you could actually dissolve into the terrain. You could be like a chameleon and with nature's makeup you could make yourself disappear.

I asked him if he could show me how to do it. He said sure. The director loved the idea. The consultant helped me do the makeup and I literally disappear while the camera is rolling. I fade into the bushes, and only the white in my eyes shows that I'm there. It's another sweet way to say that evil can be hiding anywhere. It may be kid stuff, but acting is kid stuff. It's sort of like being in the circus and you've just learned another trick.

*Surviving the Game* was one of Ice-T's first acting roles. It was right after his song "Cop Killer" had hit bad, and he was transitioning from music to acting. He was wonderful to work with—very sharp, thoughtful, and excited to be there. He had done music videos before, but he was somewhat new to film acting, and he was absorbing everything like a sponge. He would observe the rest of us and be like "Okay, you do it like that. I get it." He was learning every day, and he's obviously enjoyed a lot of success as an actor since then.

# CHAPTER 19

## IN *THE ROOM*

In 1999, a wonderful opportunity came to me out of the blue. Or more accurately, out of the fax machine.

I was on the set of a film in Vancouver. One day, I got a fax saying, "I'm Erik Leishout, a Dutch filmmaker. I'm doing TV commercials most of the time, but I'd love to do something a little more artistic. I wonder if you would consider working on this project with me . . ."

"This project" turned out to be *The Room,* a short novel by the Dutch writer Harry Mulisch—a quiet thriller he wrote when he was only nineteen years old. Mulisch is very well known in Holland and other parts of Europe—his novels *The Discovery of Heaven* and *The Assault* have sold more than half a million copies each. And Erik Leishout turned out to be a very talented director and program maker for the Dutch TV chan-

nel VPRO, and a producer for Outcast Pictures. Erik wanted
to make *The Room* into a ten-minute short film, he had already
raised the necessary money, and he wanted me to act in it.
I read the script he sent, and I thought it was haunting and
beautiful. It seemed like a nice opportunity—little did I know
how very nice it would become.

In the story, a man named Harry explains how, as a young
man, he was obsessed by a mysterious room and the extraor-
dinary piano music that drifted through its open window during the night. He would stand in the street and gaze up at the
window of that room, but he never discovered who lived there
or anything more about the place. Forty years later, returning
to his hometown after having spent most of his life abroad,
he asks one of his friends to rent a room for him. As chance
would have it, the room the friend rents is the same room
which attracted him when he was a young man. He is puzzled
by the coincidence, until he discovers the secret that brought
him to this room again—he is terminally ill, and this is the
room where he will die.

When I first got the offer, I was on the road. Almost a year
passed before I was in Holland again and able to sit down with
Erik. Once there, I agreed to do the film. From the first moment
Erik and I talked, there were many connections between us.
We both loved old black-and-white films—we wanted to do
this one in black-and-white. We both loved shooting films in
anamorphic—the widest screen format there is. Filmmakers
use it when they want to show more—like if their film calls
for wide-open vistas. Even though we had little to show in *The
Room*, we decided to shoot it in anamorphic because its wide-

ness would increase the feelings of loneliness and isolation we were trying to convey.

After trading ideas with Erik for a little while, an idea occurred to me. I had always wanted to direct, ever since those long-ago one-act plays I had done for the Noorder Compagnie. In those days, the power and creativity of directing had really turned me on. Circumstances had pushed me toward acting, but the urge never left me—all the time I was acting, the directing had been there like a little tickle in the back of my mind.

"Wouldn't it be funny," I said to Erik, "if we directed this together? I'll still play Harry, but I'll also work with you to direct the picture."

Erik smiled and said, "Let me think about it."

A day later, he came back to me. "Okay, I slept on it," he said. "Let's do it. I think it'll be a lot of fun." What followed was an incredible experience—a small event that reinforced my own feelings about how much fun it is to direct, and how good I can perhaps be at it. We shot the film in Amsterdam over a week in June of 2000. People would ask us, "How do you work with a codirector?" And we would reply, "Well, how do you have a marriage?" You do it together instead of going it alone.

The first thing we did was set about getting the script in shape. In the novel, Mulisch uses a lot of words for Harry's inner voice—and much of that made it into the original script. But the words were just too rich. You can only handle so much poetry and so much good writing—in film, it doesn't come across nearly as well as on the printed page. It doesn't sound real. Also, in the novel, the fact that Harry suddenly got mysteriously ill hangs like a sword of Damocles over the story's head. Harry has a lot of inner dialogue that says, "I felt sick that day but I thought it was gonna go away. And then I had to see some doctors. And they were saying that I didn't have long to live. Of course, I didn't believe it at first, because I felt fine, just not all the time." It works in the novel. It has a certain cruel harshness. But if you say all that in a film, people go, "Oh, all right. So he's going to die." It gives too much away.

So we had to cut. The amount of inner dialogue that we used was probably a quarter of that in the novel, and it was torture to cut it down. We also had to hint that the man was sick without coming right out and saying it—to let it unfold. Basically, we built the film up like a puzzle. Every shot has a little piece of information in it. The challenge was to hide the information in a clever way, so that at the end the mystery that we had in the beginning of the film is solved.

A funny thing happened while shooting one scene. There is a part in the movie where Harry is taking a shower, and he seems to be in some kind of anguish or pain. So I had to take this shower and I didn't really know what to do with the act of taking a shower. Big deal, he takes a shower—I thought it would be hard to make something of that.

Now, it was quite cold when we shot most of this movie, and the water for the shower was being held in a tank that was outside. The evening before the shoot, we knew it would get cold that night, so we said, "Let's just make sure that the water's not ice cold tomorrow—let's heat it up." So we arranged for a water heater to keep the water warm overnight. The next morning, we rehearsed everything except the showering. On the take, I jumped in after the water was running and almost got burned. The water was steaming hot—we had to wait for it to cool off.

"Let's do it later," we said. "Let's just shut off the heater."

We shut it down and left it there. Outside. In the cold. We continued shooting other things, and later, at the end of the day, we returned to this itty-bitty shower scene. They assured me we'd be fine now, so I got undressed. They were ready to shoot. We rolled the camera, on action I stepped in, and the water came out in a powerful stream. This time it was better—it wasn't hot like before. In fact, it was colder than any water I have ever felt. Like thirty-four degrees Fahrenheit. It was so cold that I could hardly contain myself. I *was* in anguish—and it ended up in the movie. That's what I like most about the entire film. It is a very close shave—I don't see a lot of acting in it.

There is a scene where a young Harry is on the street talking to his first love. The "first love" scene had never been scripted, but the idea came up while we were shooting. Our costume designer had been a model but was very shy about it. I got the idea just by having an off-camera chat with her. I asked her if she was open to doing it. Just one shot. No talking. It took a bit of convincing because she had burned out on being photographed.

Another thing—the young Harry spies a half-empty wineglass through the window when he is looking up at the room. I put the wineglass there to give some proof of a real life going on inside because the voice-over speaks of the fact that Harry doubts his own observations. So the wineglass is there, half full and half empty. It's a sign of life. Maybe he or she will come and pick up the glass and take another sip and greet the young man outside. The wineglass is an echo from the past—it makes the presence of the people who used to live there more immediate to the older Harry. "I felt abandoned by people I didn't know," Harry says at one point. It's a line that chills me with its loneliness.

The idea of the echo came to me because of something that happened in my life. It's sort of crazy—but while doing this film it seemed to make sense. Many years ago, a friend and I were traveling to the Red Sea to go scuba diving—the Red Sea is a paradise for divers. We were on our way to Israel, and we had a stopover in Cairo, Egypt. The next plane wasn't for another four hours, so we had some time to kill.

"So we're in Egypt now," my friend said. "Why waste it? Let's go see the Great Pyramids."

We left the airport and jumped in a taxi, but we hit major traffic in Cairo, and it took us a long time to get to the pyramids. We arrived five minutes after closing time. There was a fence outside the entrance, and a man came out and put a padlock on the fence. He looked like a guy about to go home from a humdrum day at the office, rather than from one of the cradles of civilization.

"Wait a minute," we said to the guy. "We want to take a look inside for five minutes."

He waved his hand. "We're closed for the day."

We hesitated for a moment. Then my friend stepped up and said, "Please, how much to get in?"

"Maybe you can come back tomorrow? Tomorrow is better."

"How much? We can't come back tomorrow."

So he quoted us a price, shockingly high. After a few minutes of haggling, we arranged a lower price with him. "Five minutes," the man said. He put five fingers in the air. "But only five minutes."

We ran up the stairs, and it was quite a climb. It took about five minutes to get into the room inside the pyramid. And in this room where Egyptian culture had bloomed, we found a surprise—there was really nothing to see. It was just a room full of stones, basically, and the stairway that led up to the room.

Then we heard this really strange sound, almost like a hum. It sounded like a bunch of airplanes in the distance, coming to bomb the place. *Hmm. Hmm.* We looked at each other and went, "That's kind of weird, isn't it?" All right, well, nothing more to see. So we ran back down to the guy and told him something strange was going on in the room.

He didn't seem concerned, or even interested. "No, no," he said. "That sound is the echo of the people who were there earlier."

"Earlier? How much earlier?"

The guy shrugged. "I don't know. Earlier."

Amazing. Was it a day earlier, or a month earlier, or was it from the time of the pharaohs, or what? *The echo of voices that were there*—that really hit home for me. In a way, there is ancient wisdom in that room that says, "We have a secret. If you get in here, you may discover it." I wanted *The Room* to have some flavor of that.

The world premiere of *The Room* took place on September 26, 2000, at the Nederlands Film Festival of Utrecht, in the Rembrandt Theater. Its screenings gathered a lot of enthusiastic comments from audiences and critics alike, and I knew we had something good. In April 2001, it won the Carte Noire Award at the sixteenth Festival du Film de Paris, as Best Short Film in competition.

*The Room* had a limited release in Europe, and is available there on a double DVD with *The Hitcher* and a documentary about the making of *The Hitcher*. Unfortunately, this DVD is not formatted for the United States.

This small picture is one of my proudest achievements. I feel like the acting is so thin, it isn't even there. It was nothing I planned for—it just happened as a result of how well Erik and I worked together. Now that I've made *The Room*, I'm looking for more opportunities like that—I want to direct again.

## CHAPTER 20

## BACK TO THE BEGINNING

I started work on *Batman Begins* the day after I met the director, Christopher Nolan. I went in for makeup and costume on a Monday. I think I shot my first scene that Wednesday. But on Monday morning I was in the full CEO power suit, trying to figure out what to do and how to be Richard Earle. I figured that he ran the company almost like the captain of a submarine runs his ship. He doesn't talk much—he commands with a quiet and intense authority. When Bruce Wayne returns from the dead, Earle takes it in stride. He thinks the kid will be an interesting challenge. And Earle never loses his cool, even when the kid beats him in the stock transaction at the end of the story.

The main reason is that he is a true competitor. For him, it's not about money, or even winning and losing. He's in it for the game, the competition. So when the kid outsmarts him, there's something wonderful about that. If they can beat him like that, it's not the end of the world—it's a worthy takeover.

I was mulling these things over in my trailer when a knock came at the door. I opened it and Michael Caine stepped in. He was playing Alfred the butler, and we were going to have a brief scene together. We embraced furiously and he was just as happy to see me as I was to see him. Incredible—we had worked together in Kenya on *The Wilby Conspiracy* in 1975. Thirty years had gone by since I'd seen him. Other than age we had not changed. We had the same warm and friendly feeling together that I remembered from before, just as though three decades hadn't even passed.

Another actor I worked with on the film was Morgan Freeman. Morgan is one of my heroes. His portrayal of a prisoner in *The Shawshank Redemption* is some of the best screen work I've ever seen. I was very excited about working with him. We play adversaries—he is my employee, but he is secretly on the side of Bruce Wayne, helping the kid to use some of our weapons technology for his little Batman escapades, and ultimately helping the kid take control of the company away from me. Our relationship revolves around a one-sentence punch line, "Didn't you get the memo?" I use it first when I fire Morgan, and he uses it later, after he fires me.

Getting to work with someone like Morgan is a form of excitement. Great actors give you their performance—they don't take something and they don't steal from you. They're not trying to step on your toes or in front of you, and they're not trying to break your balls. I found Morgan so warm and comfortable, and so precise in the way he almost disappeared and faded into his role. From what I've seen, the best actors are always the easiest to work with. They're private, they're nice people, and they don't fuck around.

One last note on *Batman*—the director. Chris Nolan is a young guy, and had made just a few movies before this one. Yet he's one of the most confident directors I've met. One day, we were on the set. We had to film a very simple scene—a funeral. Bruce Wayne's father has been murdered, and now they're going to bury him. We've all seen this scene a million times, and it's always the same. People standing around in black, the priest saying "Rest in peace, this and that, for all eternity. Amen." That was the scene as it was written in the script, and afterward, I was supposed to meet the child Bruce Wayne and give my condolences.

They had built a graveyard set next to a castle and it looked great. The sets on this movie were some of the most well done and lavish that I've seen, and the graveyard was no exception. But the weather was not cooperating. It was whipping rain and wind, and the trees were going up and down like in a hurricane. It looked like we weren't going to get the shoot in.

Chris said, "You know? I think that graveyard set we have is kind of boring. The whole scene doesn't really work for me. But this weather is so nice. Let's do something with it. Why don't we have a brief funeral shot, and have them all run to their cars after it's done? We can do the condolences in front of the door to the castle."

So that's how they shot it—in the wind, in the rain, just before getting into the car. People are rushing, and the umbrellas are all over the place. Everybody's hair is dripping wet. Instead of what you've seen a million times, he gives you something different, and it tells a story. It's the same story, but he tells it his way, and this time it's stormy and gloomy and nasty. It sets the mood—this kid is going to suffer.

This may seem like a small thing, but it isn't. There are 250 people on the set. And now you have 250 people going "What is he going to do? We're not shooting on the set?" It's not easy to move that many people quickly in another direction, but he did, and he did it quietly. That's his confidence coming through—people feel it and they respond to it.

Confidence is the key to everything. Some directors have it. Chris Nolan has buckets of it. He doesn't rush. He lets the actors do their thing and he leaves people in peace. He knows he's going to get what he needs. People wondered a little because the movie spent a lot of time in postproduction. When it finally came out, I think it became pretty clear to everybody where Chris gets his confidence—he's good at what he does. *Batman Begins* is one of the best big-budget pictures I've seen in a while.

\*　　\*　　\*

I made two movies that came out to a lot of fanfare in 2005— each for different reasons. If *Batman Begins* was less a cartoon than its predecessors, the whole idea of *Sin City* was to create a cartoon brought to life.

The movie is based on the graphic novels by Frank Miller. Miller felt that he had gotten burned while writing *Robocop 2* and *Robocop 3* in the early 1990s. As a result, he wouldn't sell the *Sin City* film rights to Hollywood. He changed his mind when *Once Upon a Time in Mexico* director Robert Rodriquez secretly made a *Sin City* short, and offered it to Miller as a sort of tryout. Miller liked what he saw. Finally, he was on the same page with someone in the movie industry.

Rodriquez shot the film on what's been called a "digital backlot." Basically, it's a room with a bright green screen. The actors come in and do their scenes in front of the screen, and the backgrounds are added in later. It's a technique that would lend itself perfectly to shooting *Sin City*. For the actors, all you would have with you in front of the screen was yourself and a couple of props.

Of course, not everybody loves the green screen, but I think it's great. It's kind of hilarious to act in front of it, and it can work very well. I also like the fact that films are artificial and I don't even mind that on a film like this, you really feel how artificial it is. The truth of what we do is that it's make-believe.

The shoot took place in Austin, Texas, at the facility Rodriguez has there. I was there for a grand total of three days. When you come in to do your part in a digital movie, it isn't quite what you expect—you know right away that this is something different. The set itself is so barren—there's nothing in it—it's almost like returning to the stage. Then the director explains a bit about the new medium and how things work, what needs to be left to the imagination, and how it'll all come out in the end. As an actor, you just have to open your mind and say, "Okay. I'm with you. I'll take the ride."

In my scene, I play Cardinal Roark. The character Marv, played by Mickey Rourke, comes up a narrow flight of stairs, bursts into a bedchamber, and murders Roark. Roark is lying in bed when Marv comes in, and they have a small discussion before Marv kills him.

When I shot the scene, the only things on the set were the bed, a bedside table, the book I was reading, and me. Nothing else—not even Mickey Rourke. Mickey was already done. He had shot all his scenes eight months earlier. That left me in a funny place—not only did I have to shoot a scene in a Day-Glo green room with just a couple of tools available as props, the other actor in the scene with me wasn't there.

They showed me his performance and we figured out a spot so that it would look like we were in the room together. Then they had Mickey's voice feed me the lines as I sat with a skull-cap on my head looking very much like Brando in *The Godfather*. We rewrote the speeches, and what was left I read from a teleprompter. Then we changed them a little more and I read them again. I liked working with the prompter—I found that you come in fresh and open and not so focused on or worried about what you have to say.

We shot my big scene in half a day, some small things the next day, and then I was done. I was back in Los Angeles before I knew it. I had maybe a page and a half of dialogue in the script. And what I find fun and interesting is that I think I'm able to penetrate pretty deep with a performance that is really very short. Nothing major, but the challenge is there—can you make it burn somewhat? Can you give it weight and wit and power?

I was curious to see if we had pulled it off, both the movie itself and my role in it. This kind of filmmaking hasn't been done a lot, so it was something of an experiment. I also love black-and-white, so I wondered if that aspect of it would hold up and not get boring. When I saw the movie, I was blown away. The film itself was very entertaining and audiences responded well. Of course, Robert Rodriguez seems to be out in front on digital filmmaking, which is where a lot of things are starting to happen. I think the influence of digital is going to be enormous.

For one, digital is a fraction of the cost of film. A new generation of young filmmakers who can't get themselves arrested in Hollywood—let's face it; access is still hard and always will be—will come from the margins, independently, with these inexpensive digital films.

If this shakes things up a bit, that's great. Filmmaking is a business and everyone involved is out to make some money—I understand that. But if the commercial programmed mind-set gets into the piece itself, or into your mind too much, I think you're losing the creativity and the reason to tell the story. The trouble starts when money becomes the only reason to make a film. It won't hurt to let in a little fresh air from outside.

\*     \*     \*

Another big production I worked on that came out in 2005 got a lot of attention for a different reason, and not a happy one. The critics panned it. *The Poseidon Adventure* was a remake of the 1972 film, which itself was based on the 1969 novel of the same name. This was a Hallmark film that was shown on NBC television in the United States.

We shot for ten weeks in Cape Town, South Africa. In the story as it was rewritten, the gigantic S.S. *Poseidon* cruise liner—with 2,500 passengers on board—is on a monthlong voyage from Greece to Australia when it is taken down by a terrorist bomb. The ship capsizes and rolls over. Now up is down and down is up. A small band of survivors has to make its way up, to the bottom of the ship, to escape the rising water. I played one of the survivors—Bishop Schmidt, a man of God who has lost his faith.

On the set, the days started just after 6 A.M. With a big cast, all the different actors brought their personality to the table and they all continued sketching and outlining their characters. It was a gentle and furious battle during each scene to find out where it would go—what little treasure we would find and who would find it. It was a delicate dance, and I had a ball with the director John Putch and the cast.

Sylvia Sims—who played the widow Belle Rosen—astonished me with her wit and energy. We connected instantly. No longer in her sixties, she was always there, always up, and always a great sport. I was smitten by her perseverance and her endurance—this was a physically demanding shoot and we survivors spent a goodly portion of our time underwater. In particular, there is a scene where we all have to hold our breath and swim through a flooded corridor.

Now, I stopped doing stunty stunts some few years ago—but swimming and diving you can leave with me. As we got into shooting, it was clear that certain things had to be dealt with. I had to ask for some handles I could use to push myself along while swimming underwater because my shoes were not working much as flippers. Also, fully dressed, our bodies would not easily stay down. It's all about buoyancy—divers know.

To keep us down, we all got weights sewn into the seams

of our wardrobe. Also, the Bishop was carrying a fireman's ax he was using to hack through obstacles. I had to argue a bit with the director to keep the ax. They thought I was crazy to want to swim with that. But after seeing how difficult things were "down under," I kept it and it turned out that it helped me stay down and move fast. I could literally pick at stuff to keep me going. And I must admit that a bishop with an ax (to grind with God) just utterly appealed to me.

Part of the fun dampened quickly. Whatever can go wrong, will go wrong—isn't that the rule? When we shot the scene the first time, they had heated the water. Everything happened inside these massive reinforced corridor tanks. I don't remember how many hundreds or thousands of gallons they held, but filling them and heating the water was a major undertaking. It took a whole night to get the temperature going in there, but the heat of the water started to affect the glue that was used to build the set.

In some places, pieces of the set started to loosen up. The crew had to install makeshift reinforcements on the outside of the tank, all of which took hours. Then, as we were waiting for things to be fixed, the clarity of the water started to lose its touch. It became cloudy—you couldn't see and you certainly couldn't film under there. We got two shots in that day, and it was back to the drawing board. Overnight, they decided they couldn't heat the water anymore. We had to wear wet suits under our clothes when we did the reshoot, which made it almost impossible to submerge at all.

While the shoot was great fun, the movie came out in November of 2005 to very nasty reviews. It was a monster project for everybody involved. The movie, as we shot it, was over four hours long—they intended to make it into a mini-series. The cast was a whole crowd, and as a result, all the roles were relatively thin. I felt the challenge would always be whether the drama could keep its sense of urgency. In the end, it may have been too difficult. They had to reedit it into a shortened version, cutting it almost in half to show it on TV for just one night. That whittled down the characters even more.

I'm sorry that the movie didn't come out that well, but hey, it's a living. You gotta do what you gotta do, and to still be doing it now, after nearly four decades, is gratifying. Inevitably, people ask me if I'm going to retire one day. My answer to this is that it's organic—with acting, if people don't want you anymore, you're not acting anymore. People seem to want me, and I'm still having fun. I hope I'm a better actor now—I think I am. Of course, even if people do want you, you can decide to quit. When I'm on the road, I miss my wife more than ever. My two anchors are Ineke and the work that I do. One is an emotional anchor and the other is an anchor in society, where my work gives me my foothold in the world. Sometimes there's a tug-of-war between those two anchors.

All the same, I like making films too much to give it up. And new opportunities keep arising. I am looking at directing a feature-length film in Holland—if it happens, it'll be a dream come true. It's a story of the Dutch Resistance during World War II, which is kind of ironic because *Soldier of Orange* was my big break. And it came about so easily.

A bunch of producers said, "We want him for the role," and my agent said, "Okay, who's directing?" The producers didn't have a director yet, and so my agent said, "Well, he's been directing and he wants to do more of that now." I met with the producers and struck a connection with them. Now we're working on a script and talking about who we want in the movie.

The bottom line for me is that making films is a game, and it's fun to play. The great thing is that's what I liked about it in the first place—I became an actor to have fun. After long years in this business, you come back to the beginning.

# CHAPTER 21

## A SHORT COURSE ON ACTING

When I first came to Hollywood, the first seven or eight
years, I probably didn't take it seriously enough. I used
to say to producers, "Come on, boys, this is only a
movie. You know this is a movie, right? This is all it is.
Don't get too upset about it." I wasn't willing to play the
game. And I didn't endear myself to too many people in
those days. Of course, people would get upset—they
only took out second mortgages on their houses to
make this movie.

*—RUTGER*

I first began acting as a child because my parents were actors.
This was when I was ten or eleven years old, and I was doing a bit part on a television show at the dawn of Dutch TV.
I was supposed to say something in French. It was a French
piece, and I had one line. I was supposed to say, *"Bonjour,
mademoiselle."*

But in those days, I had this Amsterdam working-class
street accent. You can think of how I spoke as sort of like the
Dutch version of Brooklynish—the way Americans think of
how people from Brooklyn sometimes speak. When the time
came to say my line, no one could understand what I was say-

ing. They decided to cut the line because it was better not to hear me talk like that.

A half century has passed since then. I have been a professional film and television actor for more than thirty-five years. I have had many wonderful, and some not-so-wonderful, experiences with my craft. Even so, I sometimes wonder if I know all that much about acting, or whether I could impart anything of value to someone who would like to learn. Consider this chapter my attempt to share with you a little bit of what I have learned.

I'm sure you know there are hundreds of ways to perform and to get there. But there are also some basic truths about film acting, and basic concepts of filmmaking that almost everyone can agree on. Once these are out of the way, there is room for making magic.

The first thing to know is that film acting is a vastly different craft from stage acting. I have mentioned this earlier, but it bears repeating. Many people can watch films and go to the theater and miss an important point—that the two forms are very different. The first and most obvious difference is that the stage is, of course, live. It is happening right now in front of an audience. The audience's response—or lack thereof—to what you are doing is immediate. It's one big go, and you don't get a second chance to get it right. If you're not happy with what you've done, you can't go back and do it again. If someone flubs a line, no one says, "Cut!" You're on to the next thing and you have to put it out of your mind. And your performance hinges on the other actors onstage—you are interacting with them in a most intimate and, at the same time, public way.

Film couldn't be more different from stage acting. You

act in a film and you have no idea what it's going to end up coming out like. It's out of your hands, and the audience won't see it until months or years after you've acted in it. Film is also a bunch of details that are pieced together. When you shoot a film, you often shoot it out of sequence. You may shoot the end first, then the beginning, then the middle. You may shoot half the movie on a film lot, then shoot the rest a month later on a tropical island or a snowcapped peak. You do the same scene over and over again, and even the scene will be shot in pieces. Many times, you do several shots— long-range, medium, close-up for the same scene. Then you do the whole thing over again, speaking your lines off camera while the actor in the scene with you goes through long-range, medium, and close-up. You are giving it the same intensity and doing it the same way as before, but the camera isn't looking at you anymore.

In some cases, you act out your role and there is no one else there. In 2005, I worked on a film in Madrid called *Goal II,* which is about a professional soccer team. I play the coach of the team. In one scene, I am supposedly at a big game, in front of a gigantic crowd, watching the action from the bench. I am speaking to the players next to me. A moment later, I am standing on the sidelines, waving and shouting at the players on the field at a climactic point in the game. In real life, there was no game. There were no players—not on the bench and not on the field. There was no crowd. It was just me, waving my arms in a vast empty stadium, pretending there was a game going on.

Another big difference between film and the stage is the type of performance that goes into it. Stage performances are much bigger than film performances. They have to be. I remember how I felt when I saw my father act on the stage; I thought, "That's way too much acting." I knew it then—it made me uncomfortable. If you're dying, you go, "I'm DYING! I'm DY . . . ING!" It's huge and it's tragic and you club everybody over the head with it. And I understand when you say, "There's a guy in the back row who really needs to get this." You need to project, and you need to inflate it. The problem is that you may reach that guy in the back, but the guy in the front is going "Okay, all right already."

In film acting, you want to underplay emotion. The camera is very close to you and you need not worry about it not catching what you are doing. It will not miss you. In my films, I want to take this even further, and I do. I hate acting when I see it. I don't want to feel it and I don't want to see it. I want to be carried away with the story—I don't want the actor's ego in front of me. I want to believe these are real people on the screen in front of me, and not actors. So when I act, I play it down. In a sense, I want the audience to do some of the acting for me. I hope that they'll be able to feel what my character's going through, and I can't get there by hitting them over the head with it. If the actor feels it too much, the audience won't feel it enough—that's my take on it.

In *Escape from Sobibor,* a television movie I did in 1987, I played Sasha Pechersky, the leader of a group of Russian soldiers imprisoned in the notorious concentration camp Sobibor during World War II. The movie is the true story of a mass escape that took place there in 1943—more than three hundred people got out alive—the largest escape from any Nazi death camp. In the story, the Russian soldiers ally themselves with the Jews in the camp that have not been sent to the gas chambers, and together the two groups plan and carry out the escape.

During the planning, Sasha must communicate with Leon (played by Alan Arkin), who is the leader of the Jews. The two men cannot be seen together for fear that the guards will suspect something. Instead, they fake a love affair between Sasha and Luka, a beautiful young woman in the camp, played by Joanna Pacula, and she relays the messages back and forth. While carrying out the ruse, the two actually do fall in love, but it's a relationship that can never be consummated or even discussed. There is no time for love because the escape must happen soon, and in any case, Sasha has a wife back in Russia to whom he has been faithful throughout the war.

The entire love affair takes place with facial expressions and with how they look at each other. It's all unspoken—the desire, the sense of loss, the fear, the yearning for a time and place where things might have been different. I won the Golden Globe Award for Best Supporting Actor for that role, and the subtle interplay between Joanna and me probably had something to do with it.

Now, let's have a word about film in general, just to keep it in perspective—film is not an actor's medium. Sorry. Everybody seems to believe that it is because actors are the ones who are made into stars. Having stars is only a marketing technique. Stars are the vehicles that sell the movie—marketers use the same techniques to sell music, baseball games, and hamburgers. But it's not the actor who makes the movie good. Some actors are very nice on the screen, but they aren't that important. They're just not.

How many movies have you seen that are terrible, and that just happen to have a great actor or a very good actor, or even two or three of them in the movie? I think I'm a good actor, and I've been in more than a few stinkers. Why, in a bad movie, are good actors suddenly not so good? And how many very good movies have you seen that happen to have actors who are normally pretty mediocre? Quite a few, I'm guessing. Some actors, you could just shoot them. Why? Who knows? It's not about their acting, necessarily. It's just that you can't watch them. The camera doesn't love them. And yet they can appear in good movies. The point is the actor isn't driving the movie—the story and its energy are.

Of all the elements that go into making a film, the director and the script are the most important. They control the action. The first thing I do when preparing for a movie is find out what the director sees in the script. Then I read the script again and again. It helps me to get its flow and melody—its pace, its rhythm, its humor. I find out where the big moments may be. I hunt for clues about the character I will play. Anthony Hopkins once said you read the script over and over again—until it becomes like a chant. You read it. You read it. You read it. You chew it. When a word or vibration is wrong, you think, "What is this? What am I missing or what needs to be changed?"

I do some research about the subject of the film. It's a good tool for preparation and it will often pay off in providing some details that may not be in the script but can give the character depth. All of this feeds me with ideas I check with the director. If I can, I like to work very closely with the director on this. As an actor, you can't see the whole movie, so you can't know how well your ideas fit with everything else that's going on. But the director knows.

After a few readings, I begin to get a sense of what in the script can or needs to be cut. I feel that oftentimes, saying less in any given scene is better than saying more. It can make what you do more intense and give it more weight. This is a very raw process. Nasty. Vigorous. I like cutting it to the bone. I strip the unnecessary words, and try to combine, shorten, condense, and intensify my lines. I have hardly ever seen a script that reads the same once brought to film. We have seen how well this can go sometimes—like when I cut down most of my lines from the final scene in *Blade Runner*. Cutting out several lines of technical jargon, and adding "All those moments will be lost in time, like tears in rain"—that's an example of when this process really works.

But cutting is a tricky business. Sometimes you can cut too much. One example that comes to mind is the film *Bone Daddy*. We were deep into the shoot, and we realized that the total length of the film would be too short. This was an HBO original film, and because of their scheduling constraints, the TV networks usually need a certain length. So the producer had a fit, and gave us an extra day. We added and shot a new scene, which added two or three minutes to the film. The scene was quite good, but not long enough to solve the problem. The director ended up not having enough material for the editor to work with.

Also, when you're trying to cut something, or change something, you can find that what the writer did in the first place is better than what you've been agonizing over. An example of this was on *The Hitcher*, which was written by Eric Red. After poring over the thing for hours, I had cut hardly anything and had really changed just three words in the whole screenplay. And each of the words I changed came in different scenes. In the end, I put two of these changes back while we were shooting. The screenplay was better the way it had been written. This is also part of the reason why I don't improvise. I feel that out of the five or six lines I come up with, three of them are terrible—and then I'm thinking about what I will say, instead of getting comfortable with the moment. Improvisation is very tricky because most of the time the writer has already done a better job. You lose more than what you add to it.

Before shooting, I start working on my character, trying to make it believable and realistic. I play with the character, adding detail and nuance. Over time, I am tweaking and rounding the character up. Intensifying it. This sort of thing is my bliss, and I usually am doing some variation of it right up until the end of shooting. Meanwhile, I keep rereading the screenplay each day, now filling in my mind with what we've shot so far and how we did it.

In 2001, I was invited to play in a movie directed by George Clooney called *Confessions of a Dangerous Mind*. It was George's first go as a director, and he made a very nice film. Funny, a little absurd, a pleasure to watch. The film was based on the memoirs of Chuck Barris, the maker of *The Gong Show* and *The Dating Game*. In the book, Chuck claimed that while he was working in television during the late 1960s and throughout the 1970s, he was also an assassin for the CIA. The script, as written by Charlie Kaufman, the guy who also wrote *Being John Malkovich*, was a hot property in Hollywood that year.

In the film, I played Siegfried Keeler, an older professional killer, a German, who sort of serves as Chuck's mentor and confidant. It was a supporting role, but one where I felt I could put something across. George and I worked together on the parts when Keeler tells Chuck about life. "No one can know you in this world. Life is empty. You're all by yourself." And I thought, wouldn't it be nice for this madman, who believes in nothing, who goes around murdering people for money, to carry a Bible in his pocket? So we did it—he takes the Bible out and reads a verse to Chuck—and I think the contradiction makes him more human.

The character is like a toy that you play with. At home you play with it a little, and you think about it a little, and get some ideas. But on the set, surrounded by the director, the other actors, and everything else, it becomes real. Throughout filming, I'm watching my colleagues closely. There's a school of thought that says you should stick with your own performance, and not pay very much attention to what everyone else is doing. But for me, I like to work off the other actors, and adapt to the energy of their performances. I will often back off my own performance a little bit, and surrender to what is happening around me. If you let go and fall in sync with the other actors, you can have a moment where something interesting can happen.

Of course, nothing guarantees there will be magic. Making movies is like wandering through a dense garden where the big moments hide. Will the big moments come? If enough of them do, then you might make a film that travels. For a few seconds, you put your arms around the world. Even today, when *Blade Runner* is shown in Russia, in Japan, in America, people feel the same way about it. It's incredible how this movie—any really good movie—transcends language and culture and time and all these other barriers that are erected.

I can remember one of the first times that an actor broke through to me. It was when I was young and saw Marlon Brando in *On the Waterfront*. I only saw part of it, on television. But I dreamed of it for a long time after that. He penetrated my mind in a very different way. There was so much current in what he did—he flowed like a river. He gave you everything, and he made you feel everything.

I never really thought it was possible to speak a language that is not about the spoken word so much, and that pretty much moves everybody in the same way. I was raised with Beckett, and with Albert Camus, who said the only thing that's real is whether you kill yourself today or not. We don't understand one another, and we never will. It was a big revelation for me that people understand one another on a very deep level. I thought we were sort of pretending to understand each other most of the time. But then people come up to me, and they talk about one of my roles and they say, "No, we got it. We got it."

I was in Cape Town, South Africa, recently, and one day I went to visit a small winery owned by a professor friend of mine who has spent most of his life studying neutrons. When he burned out on science, he went, "I'm going to make wine." I drove a rental car to his place—it was out in the middle of nowhere. We had two or three hours of talk, and tasted some of his wine. I left there around six, as it was getting dark. I was following another friend of mine back to the city. The distance is about an hour and a half by car.

As I drove along, I heard a *boom* and just like that, I had two flat tires. I stopped and called my friend. He hadn't noticed I had stopped and had driven on without me. I said, "Come back, I have a flat tire."

When he returned, I said, "Give me a ride. I'll worry about the car tomorrow morning."

He shook his head. "You can't leave that here."

"Why not?"

"This is Africa. Chances are good somebody's going to strip the car down overnight." He gestured out at the darkening sky. "They probably already know we're here."

So we had to get a tow truck on Sunday evening in the bush. We asked around in the nearest town. After a few calls, we got lucky and reached somebody. By the time the tow truck came, it was pitch-dark outside. My friend walked up to the tow-truck guy first and said hello. Then I went up and shook the guy's hand. He took one look at me and said, "I can't believe I'm meeting you here. *Blade Runner* is my favorite movie." Those were the first words out of his mouth. We were two strangers, from different cultures—practically from different worlds—and we made an instant connection through film. For me, things just don't get much better.

## THE STARFISH ASSOCIATION

Although I had done a movie in Italy with Lina Wertmuller about the subject, I remember vividly how AIDS finally hit home for me.

The year was 2000. The place was Turks and Caicos, a string of coral islands where the Atlantic Ocean meets the Caribbean. The cast and crew for the film *Jungle Juice* had taken possession of the Allegro Resort. Most of the film would be shot there. The island we were on was paradise on Earth—a twelve-mile stretch of white sand with forest on the edge of the beach, and calm turquoise water to the horizon. Most of what the island has to offer its tourists lies under that water— a coral reef surrounds the island and at the west point the water drops to a mile depth.

The big sun is always out there. The wind is always blow-

ing and the rains are wild and short. During our stay, the daytime temperatures hovered around ninety degrees Fahrenheit.
It was the hot period—off-season. Typically, the tourists came
during the winter for temperatures in the seventies and low
eighties. The beauty of the island, the resort, and its surroundings belied what was going on behind the scenes, and out of
the view of the island's visitors. Hundreds of skinny dogs
hunted the beaches for food, perhaps giving some indication.
I was soon to learn that the reality for many of the islanders is
deep poverty. That, and an AIDS epidemic, which on the tiny
scale of Turks and Caicos, rivals what is happening in Africa.

After my arrival I had to be checked out by one of the
local doctors for insurance purposes. When he came over to
the hotel room, he struck me as a very pleasant man. As he
examined me, I asked him about the HIV/AIDS situation.
Just that morning, I had read an article in one of the local
newspapers that said it was almost as bad as in Africa and
was growing worse all the time. It seemed like an outrageous
assertion to make. The doctor confirmed that it was as bad as
the newspaper said. He said there were a lot of reasons for it,
that it was very much an underground thing, and treatment
was very expensive.

He also said many on the island believed the trouble
had originally come from Haiti. Haiti—as you probably
know—is an impoverished nation with a deeply suffering population. Conditions there are brutal, with hunger
and violence widespread. In Haiti, many, many people are
infected with HIV. Naturally, many people try to leave the
country. Thousands board rickety, unseaworthy boats and
attempt to make the dangerous voyage to the United States,

or anywhere. More than a few of them die in the attempt. Well, Haiti is much closer to Turks and Caicos than it is to the United States. In the short time I was there, several hundred Haitians would arrive by boat each weekend, trying to sneak into the country.

Of course the biggest problem—on Turks and Caicos and everywhere else for that matter—is always the same. Ignorance. Ignorance to such a point that you die. For instance, in these macho territories, men and boys prefer not to use condoms. More than that—most refuse to use them. Sex is considered to gain a man respect, and the more partners a man has the more respect he gains. Somehow, using condoms diminishes that respect level. While I was on the island a colleague of mine and I went to quite a few different schools, and we put on a playful workshop about HIV. We found many eleven-year-old girls who were having sex. Some did it willingly, and some unwillingly. But hardly any of them were using, or had ever used, a condom.

Then there's that other problem—the tourists. Tourism is the main way everyone in the country makes a living. If you live in Turks and Caicos, no matter who you are, you see money from tourism. It is likely your major source of income, and this goes for nearly everybody. This puts AIDS very low on the list of public relations priorities. Can you picture the brochures? *Come to beautiful Turks and Caicos, where a deadly disease is running rampant!* It'll be a long time before we see that brochure come out. Nobody wants to know about AIDS, and hardly anybody wants to talk about it, because it's bad for the tourist business. The society has nothing to gain by pretending the problem doesn't exist.

The final problem? People who are infected have little urge to know, because there's no benefit to knowing anyway. They are unlikely to receive treatment. The health facilities for islanders are minuscule and threadbare. There are very few medicines available, and they are expensive. There is very little help of any kind. The situation is appalling. Rather than receive help, people who announce that they have AIDS are more likely to see their friends and relatives shy away. They may suffer and die alone.

As a result of what I saw on the island, I decided to set up a small foundation. This commitment became part of a shift in my life. The basic idea was to start an organization to raise awareness and support for the HIV/AIDS situation in the Turks and Caicos islands, as well as in Africa. That idea created the Starfish Association, which has become work of great importance to me. It is work that has turned me on, and frustrated me, as I have seen up close the foot-dragging of bureaucracies and the limits of what I can do. It is also work that I know has helped a few people, and that I hope can help many more people. All of the money we have raised has gone to people who are sick, and to raising awareness about HIV/AIDS. All of the money I receive for the book that is in your hands goes toward this work.

I have learned a lot since 2000. For one, I have learned that with a disease like AIDS, nobody takes it seriously until it hits home. It's in the nature of people. People don't move unless confronted with something shocking, and in the developed countries, AIDS is not shocking. In Europe, or the United States, or Canada, or Japan, or any developed country, people can have AIDS and live a long time—twenty years, even thirty years in some cases. People can be HIV positive and exhibit no symptoms whatsoever. People have access to lifesaving medicines and health care, and they can live healthy and normal lives. These are wonderful things, but the fact that the disease is so hidden in our countries limits us from taking action and bringing pressure in countries where the disease is quite frankly out of control.

In the developing world, and even in some places closer to home for us, AIDS is going way beyond what we thought it was going to be. It is ravaging South Africa and the countries of central Africa. It is wiping out entire adult populations. A 2004 study done by the Washington, D.C.–based International AIDS Trust found that by 2010 there will be twenty-five million children who are orphans because of AIDS, nineteen million of them in Africa alone. *Twenty-five million orphans.* To provide a sense of scale, I will tell you that in my native country, the Netherlands, there are only sixteen million people in total. So what you will have in Africa, and elsewhere, is a great nation of orphans. Only the problem is even more challenging because this nation of orphans is scattered across the world, and is distributed mostly in areas of great poverty, constant warfare, and governmental lack of resources or concern. According to the study, the number of orphans grows by eight hundred thousand each year, six hundred thousand of them in Africa.

It will be very difficult to care for that many orphans. If we were able to be honest with ourselves about the scope of the problem and our responsibility to solve it, if we were able to mobilize our resources effectively, and if we were able to take the massive action needed, it would still be an immense challenge. Meanwhile, on top of the very real crisis of the orphans, the problem of the disease itself persists.

We have medicines that really work, and we have the knowledge about how to prevent—or at least limit—the passing of the disease from one person to another. But these are not nearly enough. We have to get the medicines to the people who need them—not an easy task without the cooperation of the drug companies and the governments involved. And we need to make sure that people who have the disease have a place to stay—so often they become homeless, which further hurts their chances of dealing with the disease. This means we need to build facilities for this purpose. We need to create some way for people with the disease to overcome poverty and earn a living. And we need to overcome the social barriers to pursuing help.

Right now, as far as we in the industrialized world are concerned, AIDS is underground. It is below the surface, in a place where we can't see it. But AIDS is going to happen big-time. It is going to explode into your awareness in the coming decades. We all need to decide what we're going to do about it. If we look, we can see that it is all around us, and there is something we can do to help. People with AIDS need our help and they need it badly. I'll give you examples of small victories I've had while reaching out to help.

In September of 2003, I was in Romania on a shoot. And I met a man there named Mino Damato. Some men just have such heart and courage, and sometimes I get to meet them. They then have a place in my heart forever. Mino has operated a small, safe village for about forty HIV-positive kids since the early 1990s. The kids who live in that village did not ask to be HIV positive, nor did they vote to be homeless and without parents.

So we put together a little entertainment event for the kids. We had three clowns, four actors from the Romanian national theater, a martial-arts team, a makeup artist, two camera people, and a photographer. The pastry chef from my hotel saved pieces of a wedding cake from the night before and packed them into boxes. We packed our entire team into a sixteen-person minibus and drove out to the village. Once we arrived, we picked a place in the main square where all play would take place. Hug a lot and touch a lot and kiss, too—this was our basic tool to approach the kids. One of our women clowns had a race-around-and-kiss-everybody obsession, which was great fun.

Take a moment to watch the action with me: A little sad clown sits on a bench. A pantomime. He sits there being lonely and there is a giant gift box with a ribbon around it placed in front of him. A nice girl appears and pats him on the shoulder and points to the box indicating it is for him. He decides to open the box. The present is revealed. It is a small child, one of the group from the village. What a surprise. The kids think it is a small masterpiece, and it is.

Next the pieces of wedding cake were served. While this was going on the kendo warriors walked into the square. The kids swallowed their cake and got very quiet. What followed was a very funny and serious and dangerous demonstration of kendo, after which our kendo master invited the kids to practice a few moves. The kids got very into this and the clowns kept multiplying while all this was going on—the makeup artist was turning all the actors into clowns. Pictures were taken.

Hand-holding and hugs were constant. It turned out it was the birthday of five kids, so more cake was brought to a special table and we sang "Happy Birthday" in different languages.

The day was as bright and light as the weather—sunny and warm and it could not have been more perfect. The smiles on the children's faces and the way their hands would hold on was deeply moving. All we did was give them a few hours and how much did they return? Tenfold. One-hundred-fold. It was an explosion which left me stunned and exhausted.

Afterward, Mino told me something which sticks with me to this day: "If people want to do something for HIV children," he said, "then they better do it now, because the kids need it now. They can't wait."

Here's another example of work we have done. In 2004, I was in Cape Town, South Africa, shooting *The Poseidon Adventure*. AIDS is a big part of life in South Africa. You see it on the street. The country is being hollowed out by AIDS. Yet the government is careful not to talk about it—at least, not in a way that matches the scope of the problem. So what could we do, with the little bit of money and time that we had?

First we got involved with a small company there called Monkey Biz. They basically take care of three hundred women who make beadwork for the company. Most of the women are HIV positive, and the things that they make out of beads, the company sells all over the world. It's African folk art—jewelry and dolls—and the skill is traditionally passed down from mother to daughter. Every week, beautiful things come out of there, and the profits from it go back to help the women. I knew of this company because Ineke bought something from them in Los Angeles and then she found something else by them in London, and so we started to read up on them.

Working with Monkey Biz, we organized a boat outing for about forty women who have AIDS. That was nice—the very sort of thing that fits into what the Starfish Association is about. Starfish does small things to sort of celebrate, if you can call it that, the idea that AIDS is not going to go away. The message of Starfish is that AIDS is around and you can do small things, good things and happy things, and they can mean a hell of a lot to people.

Next we rode by motorcycle to bring provisions to the township where Monkey Biz is based. We got a little bit of press coverage for that, and we brought good stuff. I did my homework and brought people the supplies that they said they needed—not the things that I thought they needed. For instance, the people said that the women needed sewing machines, and with that they could make some money doing seamstress work. So we listened and we brought them sewing machines.

Then one wild thing happened—on the way back into the city I saw all these giant cranes, sitting motionless in the Cape Town Harbor. It was before they started up for the day. World AIDS Day was coming, and I had a thought. "Wouldn't it be wonderful to hang some red ribbons—the symbol for AIDS awareness—on these cranes for World AIDS Day?" Of course, this is a simple idea, and you might think you could get an answer by the end of the afternoon. No. It took me ten days to reach the guy who could make a decision about this, and then get a sit-down meeting with him. When finally we did meet,

I told the guy, "I want to hang ribbons on these cranes. I will make the ribbons. I will pay for them. All you have to do is hang them."

"It's an interesting idea," the guy said. "Let me talk to you tomorrow." I figured I had heard the last of him, but the next day, he called me back. "Let's do it," he said. "If you make them, we'll hang them."

So I found a local producer who could finish a rush job, and commissioned him to make red AIDS ribbons thirty feet high. We got the ribbons on time, we got them to the crane operator, and the workers hung them. Then came World AIDS Day. On that day, there was press in the local newspaper and on television. A photographer and a news crew went out and took images of the ribbons hanging from all these cranes. The cranes were working, so the ribbons were fluttering and waving and going up and down. It was a very eye-catching sight, very beautiful in its own way. It became like a work of art.

The next day, the caption in the newspaper said that the harbor workers decided to put the ribbons up. That was fine with me, and what happened next was even better. An international newswire picked up the image and made it available as part of their service. Over the next few days, the image appeared in newspapers around the world. And the crane operator kept the ribbons up there for a week. I am really proud that we were able to make this a reality, and that we were able to raise awareness in this way. It was just an idea, it got done, and it was beautiful.

I'm trying to come up with more ideas like this one. Ideas that are realizable, and that somehow wed the problem of AIDS with something that is beautiful or pleasurable. My thought is that if we can do this sort of thing, then perhaps people will decide that AIDS is something they can tackle head-on, rather than look away from. One idea I have is for an AIDS awareness balloon that flies over Africa, and also one that flies over the Dakar auto race. These are little things—little flashes in the eye. My wife and I also believe that Monkey Biz will continue to grow and reach more people around the world with its artwork. We hope that through Starfish, we can raise money to help them in their work.

Here's the bottom line: Lack of concern, lack of action is what gives this disease its life. We have the information to prevent its spread. And we have the scientists who can one day uncover a cure. I remind you that not too long ago, diseases like polio and smallpox were everyday problems that were going to be with us forever. What is lacking is the public pressure to solve the problem. And that is what you and I can provide. I intend to continue to make this work a very important part of my life in the years ahead, and I invite you to join me.

*Please write or donate:*

    *The Rutger Hauer Starfish Association*
    *Mail Boxes, Etc.*
    *Via Ciardi, 25*
    *20148 Milano MI*
    *Italy*

*For more information, check out:*

    *www.rutgerhauer.org/rutgerhauer.org*
    *email: rhinfo@rutgerhauer.org*

*Also, check out*

    *www.monkeybiz.co.za*

## DAY OUT OF DAYS
### *ENTRIES FROM MY PERSONAL DIARIES*

*HOME—JULY 24, 2000*

It's been some time. Whassup over here? Well. At first I spent some time on the patch of grass that I own in Holland. A couple of new inhabitants have made their homes here this spring. Two white church owls are sitting expectantly on their eggs in their basket high up in a barn. They were about to become extinct a few years ago but are doing a lot better now. In six weeks time we will "ring" their young ones but for now they are left on their own.

Them'z shy birds, and nocturnal too.

Two storks have done the same thing next door but are very happy to join our soil for worms and such during happy hour.

In the last seven years I haven't been home this long. I'm enjoying the summer, the incredibly beautiful countryside here even with the rain, which is visiting these parts frequently. The garden is where I come to rest.

I spent a couple of days in Milan and Paris. Milan was mainly maintenance of the website. Paris was maintenance for the teeth. But we also got to see two concerts as well. One was in an old church—classical music on a piano mostly woven around a wonderful countertenor voice. It was beautiful—clear and simple. The next day we improvised a picnic at the castle grounds at Chateau Chantilly, and in the evening at the Church de Madeleine, we heard the *Requiem* by Mozart. A massive church it was, with a solid choir; one of the most memorable events.

We (codirector Erik Lieshout included) have a rough cut of *The Room* and firmly believe it is very good. Now the music and effects come into play. We hope to show it at the Dutch Film Festival, ahead of Lars von Trier's new film. We are also negotiating and thinking about more of the same for the future.

As I walk my dog, me on the bicycle, the dog on and off, the dog sometimes runs into the spokes of the front wheel. She never did this before. I realize her hearing is fading. She's thirteen. Still running at a good speed though. I see a deer grazing peacefully amongst a bunch of Frisian horses. It jumps as it sees us.

In the small river I see a baby snake swimming.

In the meantime we managed to put new wallpaper in one of the rooms here and I lifted something really heavy in a really clumsy way. So today I walk a bit like a hunchback. Pulled a muscle in the shoulder. Much pain. Little sleep. Stupid.

What else is new? I rented a boat for a week. I like sailing but anything that moves or floats has my attention. We were going to do simple daytrips, but it rained Friday, Saturday, Sunday, Monday, Tuesday, etc., so we'll have to try it again on a sunny day.

Yesterday I hopped over to London to see a director for a big studio movie. A scratch-and-sniff meeting, as I call them. Hardly anybody says what they're really thinking and the art of conversation is reluctantly explored. I'm really not good at it. I ask them about the story. They tell. It sounds flat. They say they will send me a script as soon as they have one. It's multimillions on screen and no story. We'll wait and see. In my experience there are billions of dollars available for pieces of shit. As soon as the material distinguishes itself by something interesting, financing becomes a problem. *Oyoyoy*. They will not send me a script.

And while we're on this subject, *Ignition* was going to be an action flick directed by a nice director who I'd worked with before, and whom I really liked. Not a terribly interesting role. But the negotiations came to a halt because of dollar differences. Simple. They either didn't *have* the dough or they didn't *want* to pay me. End of story.

This morning I bumped into someone. It was coincidence. Certainly not on purpose, at a roundabout. They were sitting in a car just ahead of me. Nice people. Man and wife in their sixties. As they pulled up to enter the roundabout I followed and stole one more glance checking for traffic. That's when I bumped into them, gently but rough enough to shorten the overall length of their vehicle. They were shaken. So was I. He had pulled up and then changed his mind. No hard feelings. Brought my own vehicle to the shop for new headlights.

### HOME—JUNE 2000

I brought my tractor/trailer combination with me on this shoot. It was built by me for exactly that purpose and has served me well for twenty years. The day before the shoot even began I had picked up my directing partner, Erik Lieshout, who was excited about this "special" ride. We had about an hour's drive and were early and doing great. We had an appointment to see some tests and then check out the set. Not before very long, we heard this really loud bang and I knew I had blown a tire.

Changing this kind of rubber is a serious undertaking, but we have our cell phones and help is on the way. We wait. In the back of the trailer I have a tailgate and behind that a small garage which holds a Mini.

As the process of changing the tire starts to eat up too much time I take the Mini down and tell Erik to go ahead. He can still make it on time. I'll meet him later. Anyway. The tire gets fixed not much later and I'm on the road again, and on my own again.

The next day, on my way to the set, I get another flat tire, this time with the Mini. Thank God I still have my BMW 650 motorcycle in the truck. And that's my transport for the week. Rain or shine.

Early one Sunday morning, I park the truck—which is almost sixty feet—in one of the narrow streets for the duration of the shoot. Room enough as I back it in. I have some suspicion that it is going to be a job to remove the thing without damaging any cars. When the shoot's over, it's Sunday again and still early, but lots of little cars are there now.

After about forty minutes, and blood, sweat, and some serious cursing, I'm out of there. About an hour later I'm out on the road and there it is again, that funny *kaboom*.

Another tire shrivels into history. Jeez.

This time "help" takes longer to find me and longer to get the job done. After three hours I'm back in the saddle. The distance to my place here is about 150 miles. I'm five hours on the road and not even halfway. If I don't hit too much traffic I could be there in two more hours.

After another hour's drive, you know what?

*Bam.* I get my fourth flat tire.

This one gets fixed, and I do get home by the end of the day. But I'm telling you, it was a bit of a rubbery week.

### LOS ANGELES—DECEMBER 2000

After returning to L.A. and reorganizing what was waiting for me there, Ineke and I took the motor home and headed north on Interstate 15, with Telluride, Colorado, as our possible target. We took side roads as soon as we could, and headed east, just north of the Grand Canyon.

Lake Powell, Utah, kept us in its grasp for a few days. Then we spent about a week in the northeast corner of Arizona, where the Hopi Indians have had their residence since A.D. 1400. We were in awe of their simple, civil lifestyle and culture; the last aboriginals of this continent trying to survive.

As it had gotten colder and we didn't want to get caught in early snow, we decided to go south to Sedona, Arizona, where we spent a couple of days. It is so beautiful there. Then we headed west again, back to this insane city. It was a very refreshing holiday.

### HOME—FEBRUARY 12, 2001

After dinner—not that late—we are reading some. Our dog sleeps elsewhere tonight, which makes it unusually peaceful. The shy stray cat appears less shy and more hopeful—hoping for the dog not to return. We have been leaving little bowls of food outside at night.

We are listening to music. Some very recently discovered Vivaldi. Some almost forgotten John Lennon. Suddenly, my wife kills the light and points outside. On one of the seven-foot poles of the wooden fence, a white church owl has just landed. Mesmerized, we watch the beautiful animal. It has amazing energy and alertness. His eyes could be laser beams made out of black light. As his two large claws hold his body steady, his head spins 180 degrees.

What is he looking at? Then, after ten minutes maybe, he suddenly flies up. We are grandly amazed and just as we are about to switch on the light we see the stray cat climbing the pole where the owl just sat.

## HOME—JUNE 25, 2001

I spent a couple of days in Paris. I presented *The Room* at a small festival that had been pleasantly organized by the Dutch Embassy. It was a more than pleasant evening. I had lengthy conversations with young and upcoming filmmakers on the terrace of a sidewalk café next to the church and the homeless. Fell into bed around 5:30 A.M.

Can't remember the last time I did that.

Saturday afternoon I'm waiting for a call from my possible future producer who's supposed to arrive from Turkey so that we can meet. Junkies outside are screaming for a fix. It is a nice cool, sunny day. I'm doing fine until the PC crashes. Starts again, crashes again. I call my Mr. "MAC"nificent in L.A. who keeps me on the cell phone for forty-five minutes as we tap-tap the keyboard and eliminate the problem.

I pissed away some lovely time and feel like going for a walk. It's dinnertime. At Virgin's on the Champs-Elysées I find a special DVD that I need to mention. *L'Infedele*. Liv Ullmann directed it and Ingmar Bergman wrote the screenplay. These are some serious European colleagues. I've admired them for forty years. What's more, and very exciting, is that there is a short film preceding the feature—*The Room*.

Since my blind date with the producer doesn't happen I leave the next morning at 10 A.M. The drive to the Netherlands is about four hundred miles, but I will take it leisurely. I have a small Italian coffeemaker in the back. It's a great Sunday. The French seem to be out of town. I open the convertible of my awfully nice car and get into some amazing traffic. Turns out there is an air show at Le Bourget and before I know it I've driven all kinds of secondary roads.

At Chantilly I buy a baguette and find a spot in the grass on the bank of the river L'Oise. I unfold the chair and make bread and coffee. Across the water lies a smidgey little town with a sleepy square and a dead local circus on it. Three newborn swallows sail the air with their own show. Now and then a barge passes by. My lunch is soooo French. 2:30 P.M. I close my laptop and continue my trip. I'm home at 9:00 P.M.

### CENTURY CITY—APRIL 12, 2001

First shooting day on *Scorcher*. I've found some glasses that will "make" the part, I think. It's the role of President Nelson.

I have to wear suits of course.

In makeup we pick hairdo and looks. I have three scenes today. The role is written as a commander. There are indications in the script that he is more of a thinker. He is surrounded by army and navy generals. In most of my scenes I'd rather leave the ordering to them. There are many ways to portray leadership, but I'm interested in a sensitive but solid character who has no need to boss people around.

The first paces are a gentle struggle because the director is young, not shy about what he wants. He is very open and doesn't necessarily listen but it's his first day with me, too. He might be intimidated, scared, or just not ready. In the few fast discussions we have, he seems oversensitive about the written part. Although his name is not on the screenplay I figure he probably did more on the last draft than I know.

I do like to toss the lines around before I nail them. I also love cutting lines if I feel I can show what doesn't need to be said. Later, I will find out that he rewrote the whole thing, which explains his attachment. Maybe it's brilliant.

I feel it can profit by a little help.

In the script, a part of the U.S. is in a state of emergency, and because of possible dangers, twenty million people are being evacuated from the city of Los Angeles. The president and his chiefs of staff discuss strategy. As the president looks up from the map he says: "We have to proceed as if the team's been eliminated. In a city without order, chaos rules the day. God knows what kind of madmen are running loose out there."

I ask him to cut the speech and just let me do a look. . . .

### HYDERABAD—AUGUST 15, 2001

At one in the morning all airports' conveyer belts tend to look the same. In Hyderabad, India, things are different. The walls at the arrival hall haven't seen paint in a long time. The clothes people are wearing are a mix of dirty laundry, beautiful silks, and shreds.

Temperature is in the lower steam levels. It will take an hour before all the luggage has been spat out of the ragged hole in the wall, so I have time to adjust myself to this environment. The luggage is all done by hand and it is done with some concern. Most of the concern has to do with the conveyer belt. It is not well built. And it's old. Suitcases keep getting stuck or just fall off the moment they come through.

One man stops the belt. Again and again. During the breaks seven others look at each other to find out which of them will do the honors next. It seems they have been doing this a long time and it also seems they may not go home for a while.

Although most people are local and must be tired, their backs are straight. At least half of them carry a smile, and very little is necessary to make it shine. It must be part of a secret—the secret that belongs to Indian people.

I must admit I'm losing mine after the belt comes to its final stop. No luggage. There are seven other people with a similar problem, all talking at the same time to the one lady who's handling these matters. It takes another hour to get through the language barrier, the paperwork, and through customs.

*2:00 A.M.*

A drizzle coming down. Very few billboards are lit. Mostly the city is lit by traffic. There is quite a bit of it. Older cars. People on Vespas. A mom, a dad, a three-year-old, and a toddler squeezed in between. At this hour mopeds, stray dogs, people in three-wheeler taxis are on bicycles or on foot. Smoke. Smog. Most engines are four-stroke. Honking is part of a driver's skill. Never heard such a distinction in honking. Truckloads of trucks. This road moves.

I'm watching this late-night show from the backseat of an obscure sedan with shabby shocks. Not to worry. The average speed on the highway is around twenty or thirty mph. Because it is dark, there isn't much to distinguish other than headlights that appear in strange places. Half of them don't work anyway. Cows don't need headlights. They roam the highway with an attitude. "We're holier than thou." I seem to remember in this country they're closer to god, or at least related. This doesn't mean they get more room in the traffic. A few inches from each side mirror.

My driver is about five foot one. His head is just above the steering wheel. He's quiet, kind, and considerate. His English is a bit doubtful. "Fifty," he said after I asked him how long. English is supposed to be the second language. Not his, though. "Miles," he meant as we arrive at my "new" home at daybreak, two hours later.

*5:00 A.M.*

The bed is hard and pillow so full of foam it could stop a tank. It's the hotel's best room. Freshly decorated; the smell of mothballs fighting the blasts of air-conditioning.

After the first bite into curry the next day my stomach takes me for a ride. I can also pick up one of my suitcases. Fresh clothes. Mmm. Two days later the other suitcase has showed up at the airport. I'm hoping it is on its way now. It has vitamins in it and medicine for my noisy belly. And my cameras. But customs is still holding it because of the cameras. More talks. Paperwork.

The stories I've heard about India never mentioned this. . . .

*BUCHAREST—DECEMBER 14, 2001*

Have to shoot quick words from the hip again. It's too much fun not to. Anyway. Woke up like a much dirtier devil than my usual self. Too tired for soap last night or wet hair so I ran a serious bath.

God. I like sleeping with an open window if I can help it. My woman is not here. She has many cold parts, so I can't do that when we're together. Here in chilly Romania I blow my snoring clouds of breath on my own, undisturbed.

Shit.

I'm running the bath and I storm out into the next room and when I come back there's water everywhere. This happened to me before in Luxembourg. London (twice), and Amsterdam. The room I flooded in Luxembourg had one of those wooden floors and couldn't handle a nice little steaming bath. Couple of G's there. Amsterdam was more quality. I like it there. They like me too. The wool carpet did not—one could actually visibly see those little sheep shrink. Couple of G's again, yep. London was even more disastrous. They were both classy apartments, on the second and the third floor. No, I didn't do both of them at the same time. First one wasn't too bad. Just flooded the place and *splash, splash, splash*. . . .

"Hello?"

"Yes . . . Can I speak to housekeeping? I may need some emergency assistance . . . and many, many towels."

"Yes, Mr. Hauer. Don't worry, we'll be right there."

The second time on the third floor I was on the phone and they had tried to call me a couple of times before finally knocking on the door.

"Mr. Hauer. Are you there?"

I put down the phone, open the door, and at the same time hear a familiar sound. *Splash, splash.* Feel a familiar wet sock feel as well. They have towels already. Three people. Their faces are almost hidden behind it. They jump through the door and start putting them down. *Splash, splash, splash.* Another at the door says the neighbor in the apartment downstairs is okay. He's not in the apartment right now but they are indeed moving him to another room. As the water started dripping down the chandelier, where the maid jumped to switch off the vacuum cleaner, they understood it was me again.

*NEW YORK—JANUARY 26, 2002*

As we pass through N.Y. and have some time before our flight to L.A., my wife says, "Let's go to Ground Zero."

We get a cab and find ourselves on the edge of this massive grave where thousands of nameless people passed away. Cops keeping tourists away. One of the cops comes up to us while we're getting out of the car. He says that nobody told him I was coming. Could he take us around?

We wander the premises. Watch the windowless buildings which have black tarp on their side like one big concrete tombstone. My wife says she'd like to buy a N.Y. police cap. He takes us to the station and many of the guys turn up for pictures and autographs.

It is very clear they appreciate our visit paying respects to that horrible event. We are very quiet driving back. It's a small blessing to me that something small like this can mean that much. At the airport, security is enormous.

It's weird sometimes that life continues to go on.

*MONTREAL—FEBRUARY 17, 2002*

After arriving late at night, it took me half an hour to figure out the "character" with the costume lady. In my mind I was looking for a man who is a sort of mix between Dennis the Menace and David Hockney. Don't tell them. They are both much better characters than this one. Half an hour is fast; it's all I can say. I love putting looks and details together. Halloweenish. Fun. Wacky. It's period. 1971. This can only be done with a really good costume person. Renee. What a doll. Joy. She pulled out drawers full of glasses. Nice. My face is almost too big for them. There was a pair lying in a corner of the desk. I asked if it belonged to one of the workers. No. So it became mine. Or "Siegfried Keeler's," which is the character I play in *Confessions of a Dangerous Mind*.

I met George Clooney once as I was admiring two of the most gorgeous-looking motorcycles parked in the Fred Segal's lot in Santa Monica. One of them belonged to the guy who cuts my hair. The other one belonged to George. It was spiffy and brand new and the boys were going for a ride. Well, boys. Men. Because they are. Not models. Not modeled after men. I said hello. So did he. George had just finished *The Perfect Storm* then, and had never thought about directing. A book—by the way—I had tried briefly to buy the film rights to.

As we start the work together George tells me we had met around '89 in the supermarket in Laurel Canyon. Said he'd come up to me as a fan and that I had been a friendly guy. So, it's only fair to say we'd probably spent three minutes together. Here's the thing—that's all it takes. The meeting of similar minds has its own program.

*MONTREAL—FEBRUARY 19, 2002*

Day off. Last night the producers of *Confessions of a Dangerous Mind* had organized a little cast and crew get together. Somewhere on the fourth floor of a cinema complex was a huge, new bowling hall, and I attended.

Around 9:30 P.M. the place was starting to fill up. There was some food. Very nicely organized and quite unusual in my experience. I don't know much about the sport. It appears to me to be a bit like golf in the sense that most of its players are heavyweight midlifers, consuming lots of beer, and shedding little sweat. But let the Olympic games begin. It's a youthful crowd. Quite a few pretty, local, groupie-kind-a-girls in the producers' corner. I join a few of the drivers and we start rolling. It takes me a bit to get a grip, but it's good fun. My fingers are larger than average so—of course—I get a heavier ball. I keep smacking it down with the force of a bull and get a good workout and some laughs. Very enjoyable. Get back to the hotel at 1 A.M.

The next day I feel my age. My knee is stiff as a door and I know I'll have to ice it and stay calm for a week. Hate that part. Can't be that wild, Rutger. My driver helps me chase down some tricky little things I need. We do well. And I do mail and clean up the mess in my computer. I'm finally going to write down all my addresses because every time I lose a phone or it doesn't work I am in some trouble. For the time being I have a rental chip in there. But the phone was bought in Europe. Prepaid call time. It just told me it needs more money. Back to the store tomorrow.

Read an amazing article the other day in the *Gazette* about

AIDS and rape in South Africa. Called the writer. We'll meet in the next few days. Will be interesting. Now I'll go put my knee on ice. Swim tomorrow. Got a lot done, though. Good boy.

### SANTA MONICA—MAY 11, 2002

Yesterday was Friday. It was a crazy Friday. Especially at LAX.

Waved good-bye as my wife disappeared through the departure gate. It had taken hours. Shopped some groceries and worked the bugs in my PC till 3 A.M.

The Santa Monica sky is very bright and blue this morning. Hoppers at the beach. I can't sleep anymore. Throw laundry in the machine. Make coffee. You'd think that world travelers—like me—have to be very organized. Their carry-on possessions are small. And behind every button or zipper there is something handy. I'm organized, all right. Most of the time, although less anal and sometimes even sloppy. As I sip the coffee it dawns on me that I'm missing my credit-card holder. Where did I leave it? Let's see.

Hoping I left it in my tiny office around the corner. A few blocks away. Drive over. Guess what? Nope. Nada. It might damn well be at the house *swooshing* and *sloshing* around in the washing machine that I just started. I rush back outside. As the door slams shut I realize I have left the keys of the car inside. As well as the house keys and the key to get back inside the office. My cell phone is still inside the car. I can even see the spare set of car keys lying in the shotgun seat.

I decide to walk home and give up on my plans for the day. These things tend to get tedious rather than better. At the security gate I hear that the cleaning lady has just arrived to (high pitch) "Kleaheannah!" She's from Guatemala. Talks like that. She's a golden Maya girl from Guatemala—mid-thirties—with "too meeehhhnnneee chieldrann!" Sweet. As I get in I'm ready to possibly do a ferocious blow-drying job on the driver's license and credit cards. The washing machine indeed is sloshing away. I'd put a white wash in just before I'd left and set the colored wash aside. Thank god. The credit cards are still high and dry. The day is getting better. I call a locksmith. Have some more coffee. The guy picks me up after fifteen minutes. In L.A. Unbelievable. And fifteen more minutes later I have two new locks with keys on the door and this little hiccup is history.

Part of the afternoon is spent in the center of Beverly Hills—but no shopping. The dentist. I will spend hours but I'll just describe ninety seconds. The room is small. Not exactly big enough for the three people in it. I've always been going to her. For over ten years. They have music. Elevator rock today. White latex hands approach the subject, yours sincerely. A white light sits in the center of the eye.

Tiny shots pinch in different areas of the gums, left, right, up, down. Tiny drill now. *Bzzzz*. "Numb a little?" *Prrrrr.* Uhm. Almost. "Feel this?" "Hanging in there." Up-to-date anesthetics. Dentists are proud of this. "We drill a tiny hole in your jawbone. Place a plastic tiny little needle holder. Inject through it as needed. Pinch. And voila, instantly numb and number."

Heart is racing, but that's normal. Right? Great. Now you'd probably think this is where the action is but I can assure you it's just foreplay. It gets better, but I won't spill the beans. Fuck. I smile at teeth aging gracefully with dental maintenance. What an invention. So, after three and a half hours I'm driving home slowly. I'm home at 7 P.M. in bed with painkillers feeling more dumb than numb.

## VANCOUVER—AUGUST 1, 2003

*Jungle Juice* as well as *In the Shadow of the Cobra* may almost definitely never see the light. I mean none. Rumors had it the company went broke.

Geez, I almost sound like a pulp journalist. Let me enjoy the style. Other rumors had it that the footage would hardly cut together. This is likely. I remember thinking many times during the shoot—not enough coverage here. This will never cut. Or am I missing something. The story was hilarious and lightweight anyway. Comedy berserko. That's what I was supposed to be. I played a sweet but lonely fag on a paradise island who misses some grown-up, old-fashioned macho approach between hundreds of meatless twelve-year-old wise-ass drunk willies and nipples. Who then meets a retired cop played by Chris Walken who wants his daughter. Bingo, well not really. Down the drain is more like it.

I had such good laughs with Mr. Walken. Dear Christopher. As you know his sense of humor is very specific. We melted quite well there.

Defuckinglightful.

*Shadow of the Cobra* may still be in India. There were some unpaid bills. That was on the Indian side. Struggles were said to have erupted and mysterious hands made the footage change hands. . . . 9/11 happened just after that. I speak to its U.S. producer now and then. He sighs a lot when the issue pops up. *Oioi.*

LONDON—MARCH 2004

For the filming of *Batman Begins* I am staying in the London hotel that I really like. Apartment/hotel. Service is great. They know our biz. You may recall my bathtub adventures. . . . The living room is like a home. This time I have one at street level and it's almost as if I lived here. The cables, connections, and plugs have been sorted out. Stuff's organized. I spent days cleaning up the PC as well.

Later at night I get company Walt Disney would have enjoyed. Along the edge of the carpet is a mouse who's checking out the new tenant. After having taken a good look, Minnie/Mickey does a quick 180 and disappears. I'm wondering what pissed her/him off but over the next three days I get other encounters just like this one—show up, look, think, and gone. Maybe he's on his way to the kitchen. But that's one floor lower.

All week was spent in the excited "acting the part" fashion. The cameo has a good solid structure but lacks character and I was able to drift to a horizon I saw in the back of my head because the director pushed me to explore and go there. Which is always exciting and scary: exciting because you are allowed to go there and scary because you are not that secure. I found the "key" to my part at the end of the second day. That is so great as well. It's one of the things I enjoy with vigor. The "key" is all you need, after that it is about balance and refinement. Big, sensational, grand sets. Moody, art deco, impressive.

I had some smirkyness going on with Christian Bale. We have a big problem that occurs on-set. Noise. It interferes. It seems to be coming from a natural cause and I'm not talking about rain, hail, or broken limbs. We are inside on the studio sound stage in Shepperton. It's a beautiful day outside; about to become spring, but that's where it is.

We try shooting with the noise but the sound department has problems. It's too loud. It seems to come from high up somewhere. Stagehands climb up to the ceiling, between cables, lights, and set pieces. It turns out that way above us, under the same roof, pigeons are having a little foreplay. This can go on for days as thousands of dollars keep "flying" away. One of the boys figures that a blast of the loud heaters may bring a momentary halt to "lovers' lane." At least long enough to get a few takes! We try and finally we get what we need in the can.

When I go to bed that night, exhausted, and have shut off the lights, there is a new noise in the room. How to describe it? Not like the pigeons. More like champagne corks in a boxing match. X-rated. I figure it out. It's almost spring. Minnie and Mickey have decided that my bedroom is the best place to make more mice. I won't tell anyone. . . .

*MANILA—APRIL 22, 2005*

Last Tuesday I got in this huge stretch limo to go to the airport. It was around 9:30 A.M. The night before, things were hectic as usual. Contract not signed. Travel arrangements mixed up. I'll spare you the details. Anyway. Now things were looking good. I'm supposed to land in Honolulu around 3 P.M. local time. I intend to visit my friend and mentor (Erik Hazelhoff) to present him with a birthday present I found in the Netherlands. Feeling good. Airport in L.A. is a mess but for a change I'm picked up as a VIP and have lots of time. Even more so—the flight gets delayed.

Some hours later the plane takes off. After an hour flight we start to make a big U-turn and the captain apologizes. We have to return to L.A. Some malfunction. As we touch down a dozen yellow fire trucks are racing along on both sides but the captain explains this is just a precaution. The brakes might overheat because of all the fuel weight still unburned. Now L.A. is even more of a mess because no one knows how to handle or reschedule. Wait. Another plane might be found. I decide to take a break and reschedule myself for an early plane the next day. I can't get my luggage out.

It's 3 P.M. I call my lawyer. More complications have come up. Since I am back it might be better not to fly until things are cleared. I see my planned birthday visit going south fast. Grind my teeth. These things happen. More phone calls. I plan to fly possibly the next morning. Producer—god bless him—calls and speaks firm words. If I don't fly today they will take another actor. The time pressure on their side is impossible. The actor I would work with is only there for one more day.

I fly again at 8 A.M. Make a stop in Hawaii and amazingly I am able to find my piece of luggage instantly. The guy has been waiting for me and is a fan. I get six hours of sleep while the air conditioner is drying my eyeballs and get on the next plane to the Philippines. Eleven hours. Arrive in one piece but figure I need to sleep some more because I can't read anything that is on a newspaper page. I'm met by a bunch of friendly people who I may not recognize in the morning. The plan was to rehearse but I am asked if I can shoot the next day. I say of course but hear from agent/lawyers etc. that I may have to wait. The time difference with L.A. plays against clearing all problems. Okay. *Oi.* My call is at 7 A.M. the next day and after being on the phone with the U.S. we decide to handle this in good faith and work.

In the few spare hours, I spend some serious quality time with local technicians playing around with tool kits and codes because the Internet connections are not working. I change rooms. But the same thing happens again. Many modems and calls later I find out that in this country the Internet speed is 64K—for my service provider something that is known to create problems. I have some bills to pay. But I still cannot read. My eyeballs are older than I am now. The hotel is nice. The service is trying. I collapse into bed by 9:30 P.M. local and I am awake at 4 A.M. I go to the bizz center and browse through e-mails.

At 7 A.M. I sit down with the producer and we talk through plans for shooting, then we get on a small helicopter and I am happy again. What a profession. We fly out over the concrete skyscraping city—there is no doubt the country is struggling. We fly over the coastline of the South Sea and land in the jungle twenty minutes later. I shoot some video for a documentary I am making on the life of Monty Python's friend. LOL.

## NEW YORK—SEPTEMBER 13, 2005

*Tonight at Noon* has started and I was so involved for days, hours, nights that there was no time left.

On 9/11 I did have a day off and my wife and I decided to go and join people at Ground Zero to take part as quiet participants in the calling of the names. We arrive by subway, which I had never done before. It was just so deeply sad and moving.

The next moment I got a call from the production that they would like to shoot with me since one of our last leads to take part in the feature had not gotten in on time. Planes, trains, and automobiles. So we decided to grab a coffee and a small walk to Battery Park together where my wife took a double-decker bus. We waved.

I got a call a little later that I did not have to come in so soon. I thought, "Well shoot, I'll come in early." Got in a cab and sat in it for about an hour as it was trying to find its way out of the amazing traffic knot that had accumulated there. The cab dropped me at the address I had been given, but it ended up being the West Village instead of East. Had to take another cab. So all in all I had less than an hour before going to work. Or what I was told.

I was able to welcome Connie Nielsen who I had worked with before on *Voyage*, and that was nice. She is a solid actress. Solid as in gravely good. Then I waited in a chair on the flat roof of a small brownstone until I could get down below.

I knew I had to work this afternoon but it did slightly dim the pleasure since I had gotten a ticket for the U.S. Open. I knew for pretty sure I was not going to make it. I had never been there to watch a game and this would have been the first and likely only time. But that's life—things hardly work out. Just swallow. Hard. It said $195 on the tickets. I had gotten them through a certain hustler. Great. Paid $400 for each. Omigod. Yep, a possible little screw-over.

Swallow again.

Anyway, the producer walks up and says that they think they might not get to my scenes before five. "Oh," I go. "Oh well, yea. I see. I understand."

I had not told him about my tickets, but he says, "We could push it to another day."

"Coming back to this location?"

"Yes," he says, "It's your call."

I tell him about the U.S. Open and that I'd be very happy not to shoot. He tells me fine. I jump in a taxi. Get uptown to the hotel and keep calling my wife, who seems hard to reach on the airy and noisy bus. She calls me back and I tell her we are going to the games. She is excited. We take another cab to Flushing Meadows and sit high up in the crowd and in the setting sunlight as the men's finals start.

What an event. Splendid. As I break away for some water and an ugly sausage and some nasty fries, the twenty or so young black boys and girls who sell this stuff discover my face and all come up with, "O my God that's, that's, uhm damn, uhm whatziz name. What's your name?"

And another comes in and does the same. I mean happy, loud, and crazy, excited, screaming stuff. And they all need pictures from twenty-nine cameras and cell phones plus autographs for better measure. Fun. Strangeness and beauty of this life.

The game is over. We walk away slowly and drink a late cappuccino and sit next to the fountain until the masses have dissolved and now we figure what and how to get back. We walk over to some buses that are idling and ask. Big black girl does "Oh my God," again and just tells us to wait. A few minutes later a van appears and offers us a ride. We get to the hotel around 10 P.M, exhausted and excited.

*LOS ANGELES—OCTOBER 16, 2005*

The Deckard Canyon Road is a beautiful drive by day. The scenery is magnificent and changes constantly. It is a shortcut across the Santa Monica mountains to the coast. It is maybe fifteen miles long, a favorite for motorcycle riders because it is very curvy. It needs an alert and skilled rider. I decided to avoid the Friday-night traffic going back into L.A. and take this road. By night this road becomes a mystery as the yellow stripes disappear at times. The strip is narrow and drivers are likely to swerve on the wrong side. A Hummer is a wider car than most. I so enjoy that car. It *hummsss* indeed.

At a certain point on one of the higher-elevated and nasty corners I came speeding around to find two red taillights sitting right in front of me and the entire car hanging off the mountain curb—its front left wheel dangling hundreds of feet above nothing. Three people were just getting out. I was approaching them very quickly and barely avoided hitting them.

I parked with the blinkers on in this awkward spot. Got out. There were four teens wide-eyed trying to get the car back on the road. Trying to push. It was not moving. The right front wheel was sitting in some gravel. The car was a front-wheel drive. There is a technique of lifting weight and changing a car's balance which will make the traction shift momentarily— I learned that on an off-road course in Scotland. I told one of them to crawl in behind the wheel and turn the wheel the other way and be careful with the amount of gas. Then it was a matter of shaking and bouncing the car. The driver was still nervous and I saw him put it in the forward gear. Omigod.

"Reverse!" I shouted.

Another car came around the bend and had to brake the same way I did. Hairy stuff. But the next moment the car hanging off the cliff moved back. Hah. They had been close to something very nasty. I continued my drive feeling really good.

Holy cow. Life's too short anyway. . . .